The National Trust Book of

nature friendly gardening

The National Trust Book of

nature friendly gardening

Rebecca Bevan

National Trust

For Rich
Who helped me rethink the way I garden
I miss you

Published by National Trust Books
An imprint of HarperCollins Publishers
1 London Bridge Street, London SE1 9GF www.harpercollins.co.uk

HarperCollins Publishers, Macken House
39/40 Mayor Street Upper
Dublin 1 D01 C9W8, Ireland

First published 2025

© National Trust Books 2025
Text © Rebecca Bevan 2025

ISBN 978-0-00-871594-6

10 9 8 7 6 5 4 3 2 1

A catalogue record for this book is available from the British Library.
Printed and bound in India by Replika Press Pvt. Ltd.

If you would like to comment on any aspect of this book, please contact us at
the above address or national.trust@harpercollins.co.uk

National Trust publications are available at National Trust shops or online at
nationaltrustbooks.co.uk

This book contains FSC™ certified paper and other controlled
sources to ensure responsible forest management.

For more information visit: www.harpercollins.co.uk/green

CONTENTS

INTRODUCTION: RETHINKING THE WAY WE GARDEN

In Great Britain there are over 24 million households with a private or shared garden. These gardens cover almost 1,000 square miles of land. In England alone that's more than 4.5 times the area of all the National Nature Reserves put together. In urban areas gardens are especially important, making up about 29 per cent of the space. Private gardens may be small individually, but collectively they have a real impact.

Human civilisation has been built upon our ability to cultivate plants. We have been growing food and making gardens for millennia, taming the natural world to create places of safety, productivity and beauty. We have learned how to work with the soil and the weather to grow a multitude of plants for food, medicine, perfume and pleasure. Our ingenuity has allowed us to collect and trade species all around the world, selectively breeding them to enhance their taste, smell, vigour or appearance. It has enabled us to make exquisite flower borders, train trees into unusual shapes and even sculpt vast acres into picture-perfect landscapes.

Our ability to control nature in our gardens and the land beyond has been so successful that there are few wild places left. In the UK today about 70 per cent of land is farmed and most of our public green spaces are closely managed,

meaning few people have the chance to spend time in more natural environments. Many people do have access to gardens, but these are often intensively cultivated, with the aim of keeping them clean, tidy and colourful at all times. For some, gardening is a chore, as they have become locked into a cycle of cutting plants down, clearing them away and buying more.

This book invites readers to rethink how they garden in the light of the nature and climate challenges that we face. It encourages everyone to see their little bit of outdoor space as a place to interact with the natural world, enjoy seasonal change, welcome in wildlife, cherish precious harvests and make environmentally responsible decisions. Gardening this way is great for the planet, fun, affordable and better for our well-being.

▼ With a little care, our gardens can be both beautiful and great for wildlife.

SUPPORTING WILDLIFE IN OUR GARDENS

While fully enclosed and ordered gardens may once have provided a welcome contrast to the wildness of the natural world, it's a very different story today. We know that intensive farming, population growth and urban expansion has completely changed our landscape. An impenetrable, formal garden today is only adding to the places on our planet in which wild plants and animals cannot thrive.

The loss of habitat for many plant and animal species is having a severe impact on their populations. Many UK species are in decline, with as many as one in six threatened with extinction. The impact is especially severe on insects and other invertebrates, with some studies recording a loss of 60 per cent of flying insects in the last two decades. Their loss is a huge blow to the whole ecosystem, as they are the primary food source for many other species including birds, bats and amphibians. Invertebrates have evolved over millions of years and many live extraordinarily complex lives, relying on very particular hosts, creating intricate nests for their eggs, migrating long distances and metamorphosing from larvae into winged creatures. The reason for the reduction in their numbers in recent decades is not only the loss of places to feed and breed, but the widespread use of insecticides.

For many of us, this strain on the natural world casts our gardens in a whole new light. Can they continue to be places where we label many creatures as 'pests' and banish them, or tidy so thoroughly each autumn that nothing can overwinter there? Or should they become a

Nature-friendly gardening is already helping butterflies

Most of the 59 species of butterfly found in the UK are sadly declining in numbers across the country year on year. However, surveys between 2007 and 2020 showed that of the 22 species known to use gardens (including the brimstone pictured), half had been spotted in increasing numbers within gardens. A move towards more nature-friendly gardening was considered likely to be responsible for this, while conditions in much of the countryside remain unfavourable.

refuge for wildlife, a place where we can cherish the natural world and help boost the success of many species? For people already thinking this way, nature-friendly gardening is bringing a huge amount of joy and an opportunity to observe birds, mammals and insects now infrequently seen elsewhere.

▲ Brimstone butterfly on rose campion (*Lychnis coronaria*).

◄ Greenfinches have been added to the list of species of conservation concern in recent years, but can gain a lot of what they need in gardens.

GARDENING SUSTAINABLY

We often assume that everything to do with gardens is 'green' and good for the planet but that's sadly not true. As with many aspects of our lives, gardening is an activity that can have negative impacts as well as positive ones. If we dig up healthy, established vegetation to create a new flower bed, buy products grown in peat and plastic to plant it up and use tap water to maintain it, is that really sustainable? What if we don't have time to maintain it and need to clear it again in a few years and buy replacement plants?

Gardens can provide huge personal and social benefits and help connect people to the natural world, but when we create and maintain them, we should try to be respectful of what is already growing there and the ecological benefits it might be providing. A tall tree or large ivy on a wall, for example, may not be exactly what we would have chosen, but if we can embrace it rather than cutting it down, our gardens are likely to be richer for it. Such specimens have much more value to the environment than the annual flowers we might wish to plant for some instant colour.

We can also be creative about how to reuse the materials that we find rather than defaulting to buying new ones – many of these have real charm and character or can be improved with a little care. Old concrete slabs, weathered by age with lichen growing on them, can look almost like stone and be far subtler and are more sustainable than brand new paving. Broken brick and tiles make lovely edging for a border and a fallen tree trunk can be sawn into thin pieces to make stepping stones or shaped into a simple bench.

We need to design our gardens so they are self-sustaining and need minimal resources. Storing rainwater is a great start, rather than using tap water, which has been treated and transported long distances. Allowing plants

to root into the ground is best, rather than planting in containers which need compost, feed and more water. Choosing plants that are suited to the site means they will grow strongly and last a long time without endless watering or protection from insects. Composting within our gardens is also key – ensuring nutrients from the things we throw away are captured and fed back into the soil, rather than being transported long distances away.

Good decisions like these can reduce waste and avoid pollution and also help to reduce our carbon emissions. Gardens are one of the places where we are experiencing first-hand the impacts of climate change, be it peculiarly mild winters that mean our lawns need mowing year-round, storms that fell established trees or prolonged

dry spells that our traditional garden plants are unable to withstand. Let's use this awareness to galvanise ourselves into action. There are many things we gardeners can do to reduce our ecological footprint.

The way we garden can complement, rather than compete with, our natural environment, supporting and enriching biodiversity while maximising the benefits we receive at the same time. If gardeners can work towards nature-friendly gardening, together we can ensure that our gardens make a meaningful difference.

▲ Growing some of your own food in your garden or on an allotment helps reduce your carbon footprint.

▶ Gardens packed with plants of all kinds can provide a range of benefits for people and wildlife.

Ecosystem services in gardens

Sustainable gardens can provide huge benefits to people and the planet. These are often known as ecosystem services and include:

- Healthy soils and trees sequestering carbon.
- Trees, hedges and climbers providing shelter and insulating buildings to reduce heating costs.
- Trees and hedges providing shade and keeping the air cooler in summer.
- Trees and other plants cleaning the air by dispersing clouds of pollution and trapping particulates.
- Trees and other plants reducing noise pollution.
- Lawns, borders and other permeable surfaces absorbing rainwater, reducing pressure on drains and preventing flooding.
- Flowers, ponds, log piles and other habitat supporting biodiversity, especially pollinators.
- Veg plots providing places for people to grow food.
- Gardening and being in gardens boosting human health and well-being.

CHAPTER 1

MAKING SPACE FOR WILDLIFE

MAKING SPACE FOR WILDLIFE

Although ecologists don't tend to prize gardens as highly for supporting biodiversity as they do woodlands, wetlands, heathlands and meadows, gardens can host a wealth of wildlife. A famous long-running study of one urban garden in Leicestershire, beginning in 1972, found it was visited by 2,199 animal species including mammals, birds, amphibians and a vast range of flying and soil- and surface-dwelling invertebrates.

One of the advantages of gardens is that they contain a lot of different growing conditions and plant communities within a small space. A group of dense shrubs with a carpet of leaf litter might run alongside a sunny, open lawn, which could have a small pond in the centre and a border of flowering perennials. This mix of open and shady and wet and dry conditions means gardens have the potential to attract species adapted to grassland, hedgerows, disturbed ground, woodland and water bodies.

FIND OUT WHAT'S USING YOUR GARDEN

Every one of our gardens has something to offer. Even the smallest gardens contribute to a mosaic of habitats created by the gardens across a neighbourhood. Your garden could be providing the overwintering spot for the newts that breed in your neighbour's pond in spring, while their tree is the nesting spot for the blue tits which clean your roses of aphids. Flowering plants are a critical ingredient of a biodiverse garden and ponds are famously beneficial, but even if all you have is a patchy lawn you may well be hosting a healthy population of soil-dwelling grubs, which in turn might be helping to support blackbirds or starlings. If it's lumpy with anthills, so much the better – ants make up most of the diet of the beautiful green woodpecker, which is resident in Britain all year round.

▲ The song thrush is a woodland bird which has adapted well to gardens.

◄ Frogs are frequent visitors to garden ponds.

If you take on a new garden or decide to make it more wildlife-friendly, a good starting point is to look at the kinds of habitats or resources your garden offers and the creatures already present. This will help you avoid disrupting existing plant and animal communities and means you can build on what's there rather than starting from scratch. Watching from the window in spring and early summer to see where birds are carrying materials to build their nests or insects to feed their young is a lovely activity for all the family. There are many great identification guides available to help you work out which species they are. You could even join the RSPB's Big Garden Birdwatch to monitor garden visitors over a few days and contribute to a useful set of nationwide data on our garden birds. You may be surprised to know that a number of once-common species that visit gardens, including starlings and house sparrows, are now considered at risk because of their falling numbers. In autumn, it's exciting to look out for migrating birds such as blackcaps and chiffchaffs stopping off in your garden on their way south, while later on winter visitors such as redwings might come and take the last of your berries.

Sitting out in the evening might reveal another flying visitor – the bat. It's always so exciting to have these swoop by. Bats feed on night-flying insects and the common pipistrelle can eat up to 3,000 tiny insects in one night. One of the bat's favourite food sources is the moth and there are 2,500 moth species in the UK (compared to just 59 species of butterfly). Many moths are equally as beautiful as butterflies and have great names such as the rosy footman and silky wainscot. If you're keen to see which moth species use your garden, you could invite a local expert to set up a moth trap one summer's evening; the findings can even be contributed to the nationwide Garden Moth Scheme.

An easy, insect-related activity is watching which flowers are most visited by bees, butterflies, hoverflies and other insects. Eagle-

▲ Blackbirds are often seen in gardens and the same pair may return to breed there for several years.

eyed watchers might even be able to follow where bees are nesting, be it holes in the ground, walls or trees. Projects such as the UK Pollinator Monitoring Scheme, the Big Butterfly Count and Garden Butterfly Survey are a fun way to learn to identify these visitors and log your findings. Contributing data, even on our more common species, is important for conservation and could help experts recognise future changes. That's why it's always good to share your records of whatever species you spot. For help with identification and recording, there is an increasing number of smartphone apps including iNaturalist and iRecord, both of which have a verification process for your findings. You may also wish to invest in a hand lens or a pair of close-focusing binoculars, or join your local natural history group or Wildlife Trust. For those interested in monitoring ponds and the wildlife in them, the Freshwater Habitats Trust often has projects to get involved with.

Protected Species

Some gardens which have been left largely undisturbed for years may have had a chance to build up populations of certain species that are having a hard time elsewhere, so it's really important to tread cautiously before making changes. Mature trees with dead wood or disused outbuildings might house bat roosts or swift nests. Ponds might support great crested newts or other amphibians. All our native species are protected by law, some to the extent that disturbing them is illegal.

If you have a mature garden or suspect protected species are present, you may wish to draw on the knowledge of local nature groups or even employ an expert to undertake

◀ Buddleia in your garden can be an absolute magnet for butterflies such as these tortoiseshells.

▼ All bats are protected and their roosting spots should not be disturbed.

a full ecological survey. Contacting your Local Environmental Records Centre is a good starting point as they can show you what records exist for your area and may be able to recommend ecologists to help. National organisations like the British Trust for Ornithology (BTO), Butterfly Conservation and Bat Conservation Trust are also worth contacting as they may have local experts in your area or a helpline if you need advice.

It's not difficult to work around wildlife when you know you have it – a bit of careful timing and phased working will ensure established species can thrive while still allowing you to make the garden your own.

▼ Great crested newt at Sheringham Park in Norfolk.

Wildlife in National Trust gardens

National Trust gardens support a lot of wildlife and teams often commission ecological surveys to understand which species are present, particularly before undertaking major projects. Great crested newts, bats and other protected species have been found at many places.

TYPES OF HABITAT

Many of the features we create in our gardens purely for our own benefit are happily adopted by wildlife because they offer similar benefits to a habitat which occurs in the wild. An evergreen hedge, for example, might have been planted primarily to screen a front garden from a road, but it can also provide a perfect thicket for a dunnock to nest in. A drystone wall, built to retain one level of the garden from another, may have just the right damp crevice for an overwintering toad.

▼ Blackbirds often nest in gardens and may use moss from the lawn to line their nests.

Other features could be more useful to wildlife if given a few improvements. A garden pond, for example, will be far better for supporting frogs, newts and insect life if there are no fish eating their young and raising the nutrient levels. The grass beneath your apple tree could support native plants such as cowslips, and native insects such as grasshoppers, if left to grow long over summer rather than mown routinely.

There are also a number of unexpected and occasionally inconvenient spots that can act as hiding or nesting places – the eaves of buildings, garden sheds, underneath decking, bonfire piles, compost heaps, woodstores, the dry soil in pots or between paving slabs. With a bit of care and knowledge (and occasionally specialist advice), it's usually possible to leave these undisturbed until the resident species hatch out or move on, or – if absolutely necessary – relocate the inhabitants to somewhere equally suitable.

Lawns

Lawns sometimes get a bad press, criticised for being a monoculture that is bereft of life. This is not entirely fair, however, and for many gardeners, short grass is a great option for part of the garden, allowing you to have an area which is soft underfoot and kept open, without the need for paving or gravel. A permeable surface

is better for absorbing rainfall than a hard one and even short grass offers places for birds and mammals to forage for ants, worms and grubs, or bats to catch craneflies and moths which have emerged from the soil.

If you want short green grass year-round for walking, sitting or playing on, there are ways of caring for it that can make it more nature-friendly. Don't make it any bigger than it needs to be, and make sure you have plenty of taller, flowering plants elsewhere. Aim for a natural-looking sward rather than bright green stripes and steer clear of weedkillers, moss killers and pesticides that can harm the many organisms that live in a healthy soil beneath turf. Try to see occasional holes or bare patches as a welcome sign of life that will soon grass over and simply tread unwanted hummocks down occasionally. Lawns are tougher than you think and can recover from periods of drought on their own without the need for regular watering.

In recent years a campaign known as No Mow May run by the charity Plantlife has encouraged people to stop mowing their lawns for a while and see what happens. Most lawns which are not treated with weedkiller contain a number of small flowering plants such as daisies and clover and not mowing allows them a chance to flower and offer their nectar and pollen to insects. This can be really attractive and leads some people to convert their lawns into permanent meadows. However, for those wanting a lawn, leaving grass for a whole month in spring when it's growing quickly can result in a very thick lawn, too much for many mowers. Another approach, which allows plant species in lawns to flower and yet still keeps things manageable, is to leave areas of the lawn for two to three weeks in

▶ A well-mown lawn, like this one at The Courts Garden, Wiltshire, invites you to walk into the very heart of a garden and sets the stage for its shrubs, trees and flower borders.

Lawn 'weeds' to love

Many low-growing plants can live among grasses, tolerating having their heads cut off from time to time and flowering when they get the chance.

◀ **Daisies (*Bellis perennis*)** Ubiquitous little flowers which give lawns a lovely cottage garden feel.

◀ **Yarrow (*Achillea millefolium*)** Usually very tall, this yarrow will adapt to life in a lawn by flowering on much shorter stalks.

◀ **Red clover (*Trifolium pratense*)** Provides lots of nectar for insects and fixes nitrogen into the soil with its roots, feeding your lawn.

◀ **Self-heal (*Prunella vulgaris*)** Charming violet flowers appear in summer and autumn if you don't mow too short.

◀ **White clover (*Trifolium repens*)** The classic clover of lawns helps make them soft underfoot and stay green all year round.

◀ **Bird's-foot trefoil (*Lotus corniculatus*)** A very cheery wildflower loved by bumblebees and other insects.

rotation throughout the year. The nectar will be welcomed by insects at almost any time of year.

If you do this, you may be surprised what appears, especially if your lawn is on a site that has been relatively undisturbed for a long time. You may even find rare species such as orchids and shiny waxcap mushrooms. If you get a lot of larger weeds like docks, thistles and sorrel, or if dandelions and hawkbits seem to be multiplying too fast, simply use a hand fork when the soil is moist to loosen them and then pull out the unwanted plant with its long tap root attached. This can be just as effective as weedkiller on deep-rooted plants and won't leave a shrivelled dead plant behind.

▲ Lawns at Scotney Castle, Kent, are filled with rare green-winged orchids in spring so mowing is always held off until summer.

Case study: Varying lawn-cutting at Bateman's

The lawns at Bateman's in East Sussex contain white clover, bird's-foot trefoil and self-heal, so the team have altered their mowing to allow these species to flower and provide forage for bees. The mower height is raised and the lawns are mowed one area at a time each fortnight so that there are always some plants in flower. The lawns are still short enough for visitors to walk over but monthly bumblebee surveys have found hundreds of worker bees are benefitting from this approach.

Meadows

Meadows are simply a mix of grasses that are allowed to grow tall and produce seedheads with perennial wild flowers growing among them. The flowers offer nectar and pollen to flying insects while the long grass and wildflower foliage provides food for caterpillars and grasshoppers. The dense tangle of stems also offers places for other creatures to hide and hunt, while also allowing access to the soil for egg-laying. Much of Britain used to be covered in meadow cultivated for traditional grazing by sheep and cows and, as a result, many native species are adapted to them. The change to rich ryegrass with no wild flowers favoured by modern farming has led to a 97 per cent loss in lowland

Choosing a meadow mix

A huge number of very different seed mixes are sold as 'meadow' or 'wildflower' mixes, so do your research carefully or ask for advice from an expert. Look for a mix of perennial native flowers suited to your site and soil, ideally harvested locally. You do not need annuals (which will only last one year) or non-natives (which may not form the right community). You will need a high proportion of grass seed in your mix if you are sowing a new meadow on bare ground but won't need any if you are trying to establish flowers within existing grass.

meadows since 1935, contributing to the massive decline in insect populations. Meadows in our gardens can help address this – there are species such as field and meadow grasshoppers and meadow brown and gatekeeper butterflies, which

▲ A path is mown through the long grass and ox-eye daisies in the orchard meadow at Greys Court in Oxfordshire.

will breed in small meadows in gardens but would never be attracted to lawns, even those left to get a little longer between cuts.

Converting a lawn to meadow can instantly make it more wildlife-rich and cut down on mowing while giving your garden a softer, more romantic look (especially if you mow a winding path through). It's best suited to quite large areas like orchards but many people are making mini-meadows in smaller gardens.

The key to a floriferous meadow is grass that is not too vigorous, allowing a good mix of other plants to flourish among it. To convert a lawn to a meadow, as mentioned earlier, you can simply leave your lawn to grow long in spring and summer and see what flower species are already there. If you're lucky, this may result in fairly nice effect in the first few years. If it is just vigorous grass with no wild flowers, you'll need to create some bare patches for flowers to become established, either by digging out clumps of grass or unwanted docks, or by using a strimmer to scalp it here and there. Introduce perennial meadow flowers in the bare patches, either by scattering seed or planting small plants. Many places now sell small, British-grown wildflower plugs of plants such as ox-eye daisies, scabious and knapweed for this purpose, which can be posted to you. If you want to try

introducing yellow rattle – a plant that can help to weaken the grass slightly to the benefit of wild flowers – this is best done from seed sown as fresh as possible from July to September. For advice about how and when to cut meadows so that they support the most species possible, see Chapter 4, page 114.

Sunny Flower Borders

A border filled with many different flowering plant species that bloom in succession for several months is not completely akin to anything that would be found in nature but it is usually a big hit with flying insects that feed on nectar. A Royal Horticultural Society (RHS) research project, which studied plots planted with either native, near native or exotic plants to compare their attractiveness, found that all attracted a wide range of invertebrates with pollinating insects being the largest group.

Research by Sussex University into one of our most well-known pollinating insects – the bumblebee – found that some were travelling up to 4 kilometres from their nests in the Sussex countryside to feed on flowers in gardens.

Including winter- or early spring-flowering plants such as snowdrops, hellebores, crocus, narcissus and lungwort in your borders is attractive and will also maximise their value to pollinators emerging in spring. Some species,

▲ Attractive borders like these at Castle Drogo in Devon have nectar-rich plants in flower for many months of the year – the alliums in May and June are especially popular with bees.

◄ Borders such as this one at Quarry Bank in Cheshire can be really colourful and structural as well as offering a wealth of food and hiding places for insects.

▶ Perennials such as echinacea, seen here in the borders at The Vyne in Hampshire, provide lots of nectar for bees, butterflies and other insects in late summer.

▼▼ Sunny gardens filled with a variety of plants, which have a range of structures and flower at different times, will be attractive to many creatures.

including buff-tailed bumblebees and hoverflies, will be active during mild spells in winter and need to forage. Equally, late-flowering plants such as persicarias, asters and sedums are great to extend the season after the big summer show. Whenever you're adding a new plant to your border, look for species known to be good for pollinators. This information is now widely available and you'll find a very wide range of suitable flowering plants with different heights, structures and colour.

In addition to nectar and pollen provision, flower borders also offer a mass of different stem structures and foliage types, which may be food for herbivorous insects and provide safe places for other invertebrates and small mammals to hunt and hide. Creatures such as woodlice and millipedes, which live on the soil surface and help to recycle dead plant material, are frequently found in borders, adding to their biodiversity. Leaving vegetation standing from autumn through winter until the milder weather returns is ideal to maximise the cover and can also provide winter interest and seeds for birds (more advice on this in Chapter 4, page 122).

Trees, Shrubs and Climbers

If you have a small garden, you might think you don't have space for big plants, but small trees, large shrubs and substantial climbers have a place in every garden as they fill the vertical

▲ If all you have is a patio or balcony, collections of containerised plants filled with nectar-rich flowers that bloom at different times of year can also act as a magnet/smorgasbord for pollinating insects.

space, hugely increasing the biomass. They are great for humans, providing shelter from wind and a sense of maturity that smaller plants cannot and they are great for wildlife, massively increasing the resources available for feeding, breeding and sheltering. Research carried out by the Biodiversity in Urban Gardens in Sheffield (BUGS) project in 2001 and 2008 showed that the number of trees and the area of canopy vegetation more than 2 metres above the ground have some of the biggest positive impacts on biodiversity.

The mix of woody species we generally plant in gardens, and the high proportion of evergreens we include is quite different to that which is found in the wild, but it can offer a wealth of resources, including year-round cover, winter flowers stuffed full of nectar, nuts and berries in the autumn, crevices in bark, and shady, undisturbed ground enriched by leaf litter. You can add to this by allowing climbers to twine through your shrubs, underplant them with shade-tolerant spring flowers such as snowdrops, violets or lungwort, and perhaps build a log pile nearby. It's also a good idea to put up nest boxes designed for hole-nesting birds such as blue tits and great tits to mimic the cavities they might choose to nest in within mature trees. If a bird doesn't use it, a tree bumblebee might!

▼ Attaching nest boxes to your trees can help provide habitat for many species, including blue tits which would naturally nest in cavities.

For bird-lovers, shrubs and trees that stand above other vegetation are an absolute must. Without them nearby, it is very unlikely you will be able to attract many birds into your garden, even if you have a bird feeder. This is because most birds need safe perching places with cover from which to survey what's on offer and where the risks lie. Your trees, shrubs and dense climbers may also provide nesting opportunities for common garden birds like blackbirds and robins and, other less familiar visitors, such as spotted flycatchers and goldcrests. In spring, when birds are feeding their young, these larger woody plants are likely to host the caterpillars, aphids and other nutrient-rich insects they need to find. In autumn a range of bird species will take advantage of the berries your shrubs and trees provide.

If you already have trees in your garden, it pays to be sensitive about their pruning. Most garden and street trees are closely managed, meaning few contain any dead wood. This is a huge loss to many beetles and other insects that feed on rotting wood, and birds and bats which use the holes, cracks and loose bark within trees. So,

Berrying trees and shrubs for birds

Different bird species tend to favour different fruit, but generally red and orange berries that are small so birds can grab and go are the most popular. If you want lots of visiting birds, it pays to have a mix of plants with berries which will be available over several months.

Elder Berries are soft and ripen early and are very popular with many birds, including migrant species getting ready to head south for winter. Other early ripening plants include guelder rose, blackberry, honeysuckle and amelanchier.

Rowan A mid-autumn ripener popular with a huge range of birds both resident and visiting. Other species that provide abundant fruit at this time include pyracantha and berberis.

Ivy Very hard berries which hang on late and are especially valuable to birds visiting our gardens in winter when food sources elsewhere may have run out. Other longer-lasting fruits include holly berries, sloes, haws and rosehips.

▼ Long-tailed tits use lichen, moss and even spider webs to build their nests, which are usually hidden in dense vegetation.

▶ Privet hawk-moth caterpillar.

before you pick up the phone to a tree surgeon, or pick up that saw yourself, think about whether it's safe to leave some. Most wounds to a branch can be healed by the plant itself and most areas of dieback are not a sign of a disease likely to spread. Ivy growing up mature trees is also commonly removed. It may not be ideal for a young or weak tree but most mature specimens can cohabit just fine and it massively enriches the habitat for insects, bats and birds. Similarly, if you have mistletoe, moss or lichen on a tree, try to cherish it as an extra species that contributes to the complexity of habitat. Mistletoe is an important food source for mistle thrush, whose numbers are in decline.

Hedges

Hedges are a great way to cram a number of trees and shrubs into a small area. Although they take up a bit more space than a fence, they make for a much more interesting boundary while providing some of the best wildlife habitat. They can link gardens together or connect them to the wider landscape, allowing creatures such a hedgehogs and dormice to travel safely to forage more widely and breed. All sorts of common garden hedges made from privet, box, yew, berberis, etc., may provide nesting sites for birds. Berberis flowers also provide nectar and pollen in spring and berries in autumn. Privet can attract spectacular privet hawk-moths, as their enormous caterpillars feed on its leaves.

If you have space for a boundary which is a bit thicker and wilder, a wildlife hedge made of native species is worth considering. Ideal species include guelder rose, hawthorn, blackthorn, hazel and holly, which together will offer nectar, pollen, berries, nuts and dense cover for wildlife. It is usually best to avoid wild roses in small gardens as they are very hard to manage, but honeysuckle allowed to weave through a hedge will work well,

and is especially valued by dormice. Plants should be about 45 centimetres apart for a nice dense hedge, ideally planted in two staggered rows (to make a hedge that will eventually be at least 1.2 metres deep) or just one row if you're short of space. To keep hedges under control at around 1.8 metres tall, they'll need cutting every one to three years but, for maximum wildlife value, don't prune too hard and wait until February so that berries are left on all winter.

The base of hedges is also very good habitat so don't be inclined to keep them too tidy. While newly planted hedges are probably best kept free of ivy or very vigorous grass, once they are established letting them get a bit wild is no bad thing. Small mammals like mice, voles and hedgehogs will benefit from this cover and small birds such as wrens, robins and dunnocks, which tend to nest low down in a hedge, need plenty of cover to hide from cats and other predators. A number of bumblebee species, including the aptly named garden bumblebee, might even adapt an abandoned mouse nest at the base of a hedge; you could help mimic this by burying a small upside-down terracotta pot there, partly filled with some dry moss.

Log Piles, Brash and Other Debris

One of the most important types of habitat in a garden is the piles of debris made from the materials we leave lying about – usually prunings and other organic materials, but sometimes stones, bricks or old tiles. Most gardeners will be aware that these materials soon attract life and that if they are disturbed, many species can be seen running for cover, including tiny spiders, harvestmen, woodlice, mites, springtails, centipedes, millipedes, beetles, baby newts and more. It's easy to overlook these animals but they play a very important role in our gardens' ecosystems. Piles left for a long time with rotting wood in contact with the ground are especially interesting to peer at. Did you know that at least five different species of woodlice and 420 different beetles are commonly found in gardens?

Slow-worms are a classic find when lifting an abandoned slab; newts and toads love the cool crevices between stones; while a fragile overwintering peacock butterfly might be found in a warm, dry place where you keep your spare pots. Compost heaps and bonfire piles are also popular hiding places. Hedgehogs often try to hibernate in a bonfire pile or give birth in a compost heap. Grass snakes also love the warmth of a compost heap for laying eggs.

Armed with this understanding, nature-friendly gardeners need to do two things. First, let's not create piles, leave them undisturbed for weeks, months or even years and then suddenly tidy them up or set them on fire! If you must move piles, try to not to do it between November and March when the residents might be too cold, sleepy or hungry to easily relocate. If we must have bonfires, let's always move the materials to a new piece of ground on the day they are to be lit, check carefully before lighting and leave an escape route by lighting from one side.

▲ Hedgehogs need safe, dry undisturbed hiding places in gardens.

Making wildlife habitats from wood and debris

Creating permanent features with logs, bamboo and branches is key to nature-friendly gardening. It is a great way to utilise waste products, save trips to the tip, and reduce the use of a shredder or the need for bonfires. It can also add a lot of character to a garden.

◄ **Insect hotels** A mix of different natural materials will provide crevices for a number of insects to hide. Many designs have bundles of bamboo or wood with narrow holes drilled in them to attract solitary bees. Holes of 8 millimetres and some smaller are best. Erecting a number of small hotels around your garden is likely to be better for bees than creating one big one as encouraging lots of them to nest in the same place each year can lead to health problems. Insect hotels for bees are usually best sited in the sun, raised between 50 centimetres and 3 metres off the ground, and kept dry. If the nesting material becomes wet it can adversely affect the insects inside.

◄ **Log pile** Place a mix of logs and branches at the back of a border. Wood from deciduous trees is best and you can add thinner prunings on top. Partially burying some of the wood will encourage it to begin rotting, which will help to attract beetles, including the rare but magnificent stag beetle. Log piles in the shade are likely to rot faster but piles in the sun have value for creatures like solitary bees.

◄ **Hibernacula** Logs and stones loosely piled together in a hole or on damp ground with a layer of turf over the top can create the perfect moist but airy conditions for newts to spend winter. Organisations like Froglife offer detailed instructions on how to build them.

◄ **Dead hedge** Vertical stakes with prunings piled in between can be designed to screen a compost heap or bin store. A brilliant way of providing instant connectivity between one habitat and another, perhaps beyond your garden boundary.

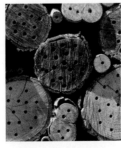

◄ **Log wall** Logs cut to similar lengths and piled within a frame. Looks really neat and architectural and can form a screen or wall. Holes drilled into the logs can help with habitat creation. Over time they will begin to rot, but don't be in a hurry to replace them as rotting wood has such good value for biodiversity.

Walls and Buildings

Our homes, outbuildings and garden walls
provide great habitat for a range of creatures.
Older buildings especially tend to have cavities
that are accessible to wildlife, whereas modern,
well-insulated homes and garden buildings
provide fewer opportunities. Whenever you
install garden buildings or features, try to view
them as an opportunity to incorporate areas
for wildlife. Something as simple as drilling
horizontal holes of different sizes ranging
between 2 and 10 millimetres wide and at least
15 centimetres deep in fence posts can provide
habitat for mason bees. At the other end of the
spectrum, using low drystone walls or gabion
baskets filled with stone to retain levels is far
more nature-friendly than solid concrete ones. In
the UK more than 8,000 kilometres of drystone
walls have been lost in the countryside since the
middle of the last century as a result of changes
to land management, and with that comes loss
of habitat for voles, reptiles, frogs, toads, a wide
range of invertebrates, some hole-nesting birds
and hibernating bats, as well as surfaces on
which lichens, mosses, liverworts and ferns can
grow. If you plan to make changes to an existing
building, especially filling cavity walls or works
to the roof, it may be wise to get a survey done
so that you can plan work to cause minimum
disturbance. Some of the species that use these
cavities, including bats and nesting birds, are
protected by law.

A range of bird species like to nest against
buildings, including jackdaws, house sparrows,
black redstarts, starlings, spotted flycatchers,
swifts, swallows and house martins, as well as
barn owls in country gardens and pigeons in
the city. Even cliff-dwelling and coastal birds
such as gulls, fulmars and peregrine falcons
have adapted to man-made ledges and nooks.
The house sparrow is exclusively found around

▲ ▶ The walls and buildings of many National Trust gardens are popular with birds including wagtails and sparrows.

buildings, nesting in loose colonies under the eaves, in wall cavities or in ivy. They were once very common birds but suffered a sudden and serious decline in the 1990s, partly due to tidier gardens and farmyards, which have reduced the availability of insects – the key food for their chicks. Starlings that were once abundant are having a hard time in the countryside due to changes in farming so our homes and gardens are playing an increasingly important role in their survival. Swifts are also highly dependent on man-made structures, nesting between roof tiles, under the eaves, in ventilators and in other small cavities. Swift numbers have dropped to a critical level (a 60 per cent loss since 1995), so if you introduce swift boxes and can encourage a pair arriving from Africa in spring to nest against your house wall, you're making a real difference

Nest boxes for house-dwelling birds

To compensate for a lack of accessible crevices in your home, you can put up boxes to help many birds which like to nest in buildings. It's best to target species you know are in the area, using your home or nearby buildings, rather than trying to attract a new species in to compete with an existing one. House sparrows need a small box with a neat, round hole; starling boxes are larger, with a wider hole, while swift boxes (pictured) are wide and shallow with a small hole close to the bottom. In general, you should position these kinds of nest boxes at least 3 metres high on a north or east aspect, so that it's not too hot and sunny, and away from the prevailing wind. Under the eaves is perfect. Ideally put them up in groups of three or more as most of these birds live in colonies. Sparrow boxes can be bought as terraces.

to conservation. Spotted flycatchers also winter in sub-Saharan Africa and return to the same nest site each year and they too are in serious decline. They like to nest in the vegetation on walls and are mostly only found in large gardens with buildings set among mature trees.

Bats are another amazing creature that have lost so many of their natural roosting and feeding places, and some of the 18 British native species are now partly or entirely dependent on buildings to provide the dry, dim conditions and the right humidity and temperature. Some species of bat use external crevices and gaps to roost in; others use small holes to reach interior spaces where they can roost as a colony. Most bats are found in older, traditionally constructed buildings, so if you have one of these it is safest to assume that it will be used by bats and invite your local bat group to do a survey and advise you if you are planning alterations. If you're in a modern house, checks may also be worthwhile as tiny pipistrelles can roost in soffits, cavity walls, around window frames and under roof tiles or felt.

If you want to provide habitat for bats, you can introduce ready-made bat boxes or make your own. Bat boxes are designed to allows bats to enter from beneath and need to be placed on buildings, trees or posts at least 4 metres high with shelter from strong winds and near linear features, such as a building, tree line or hedgerow, by which many bat species will navigate. Seek advice on the right design and precise position as this will vary depending on the species you are hoping to attract.

Many other species also make good use of buildings. Hedgehogs and foxes may take up residence in the quiet, dry spaces beneath sheds and other outbuildings. Hedgehogs might use these to give birth and raise their young,

▶ Bat boxes can be attached to trees or buildings and look different from bird boxes because bats enter them from underneath.

which happens in summer and autumn, or to hibernate, which they do from November until March, so it's best to leave them undisturbed all year. Inside dark, frost-free sheds and log stores it's common to find overwintering moths, butterflies and ladybirds. Try to leave these undisturbed too.

Many bees and wasps interact with buildings, attracted to the dry, dark conditions they provide. Most can be lived with – even the famous common wasp, which so many people are scared of, plays an important role in our ecosystem and its magnificent nests are only active for one summer. Mason bees frequently utilise man-made structures, favouring sandstone walls and soft mortar to which they do no harm. The females live brief and solitary lives, during

which they can make a nest in your wall with a number of eggs laid in individual chambers lined with mud and provisioned with food for the larvae to eat when they hatch after several months. If you notice activity around a hole in a wall, don't panic – just sit and watch the fascinating comings and goings of these hard-working creatures.

Open Ground

Bare but undisturbed ground that drains well, remaining fairly warm and dry, is one of the least common habitats in gardens, and is needed by several species which would naturally colonise open, sunny banks and heathland. In our gardens these bare patches sometimes occur in gaps

between paving slabs, containers or a worn patch on a lawn, and we shouldn't rush to cover these over. Look closely and you might see small holes where ground-nesting bees or wasps have made their burrows. There are around 65 species of mining bee in the UK, many of which are having a difficult time. Eggs are usually laid in summer, in individual chambers within a burrow, each provided with pollen for when they hatch. The

offspring don't emerge until the following spring and then need to mate and make new burrows, so sites like this are best left undisturbed all year round. In her 30-year study of her small garden in Leicestershire, ecologist Jennifer Owen observed she only had aerial nesting bees and wasps because her soil was not sandy enough and was frequently disturbed by cultivation.

Other creatures attracted to open areas include ground beetles, spiders and, of course, ants (which admittedly can be annoying at times but provide a valuable food source for other species). You may even be lucky enough to spot mason

▲ Common lizards are sometimes seen in British gardens such as Stoneywell in Leicestershire.
◄ Tawny mining bee emerging from a burrow in the sandy soil at Sheringham Park, Norfolk.

bees or house martins collecting mud for their nests. If you're really fortunate and have just the right conditions, your garden could attract common lizards or other cold-blooded species, which rely on basking in the open for energy.

Dry gardens in which sun-loving, drought-tolerant plants are grown in free-draining soil can provide some of these opportunities while still being highly attractive. These areas are usually mulched with gravel, which is not ideal for wildlife, but you could vary this with some stones, areas of different-sized gravel, grit and sharp sand plus a few completely bare patches. This environment is great for allowing plants to set seed and create natural looking combinations with minimal disturbance. You'll need to gently weed out the ones you don't want to maintain a good balance of species with plenty of open areas. Plants which set seed nicely without being too dominant include sea holly, mullein, Californian poppies, rose campion and *Dianthus carthusianorum*. *Sisyrinchium striatum* is great too but may need a little controlling. There are many shrubs and perennials that will thrive in this environment and offer nectar and pollen but will not self-seed, including bearded iris, rock roses, phlomis, ballota and gaura (*Oenothera lindheimeri*).

If your garden has no sunny space to create habitat like this, you could try filling a large container with a mix of soil and sharp sand and plant it up sparingly to see what it attracts.

▶ Dry gardens in which sun-loving, drought-tolerant plants grow in free-draining soil can be very attractive; the Delos garden at Sissinghurst in Kent is a great example.

Water

Creating or maintaining a pond for wildlife is a real joy and one of the best things you can do in a garden to boost biodiversity. Over 3,800 invertebrate species need fresh water to complete their life cycle and ponds can play a critical role in supporting some of these species, which in turn provide food for other creatures in the wider landscape. In the last 50 years over half of all ponds have been lost from farmland meaning that any we create in our gardens are all the more precious, especially if they can help form

◄ The author's pond in Gloucestershire was only created in 2021 but attracts newts, frogs and several species of dragonfly.

▼ Wildlife ponds come in all shapes and sizes. Larger ponds, like this one at Hare Hill in Cheshire, look spectacular and can accommodate a wide range of creatures.

a network that species such as newts can move between.

Anyone who has already introduced water to their garden will have seen how remarkably quickly diving beetles, water boatmen, water skaters, caddis flies, toads, frogs, newts and more can colonise it, even in relatively built-up areas. Dragonflies and damselflies are among the most charming visitors and your garden pond can attract around 15 different species, which will be very active around the pond in spring and summer mating, and laying eggs on the water surface or pond margins. The larvae of these are some of the most voracious predators in the insect world and some species will live in the pond for up to three years, before crawling up a stem and emerging from their old skin with a magnificent pair of wings. It's this rich web of life in a pond

that makes it very important to be sensitive about how you manage an existing body of water (see Chapter 4, page 134).

If you wish to add water to your garden and it is very small, even an old sink or half-barrel sunk into a border can attract wildlife. However, wildlife ponds are typically bigger – with at least one gently sloping side so wildlife can get in and out, and some shallows so that birds can bathe, insects and newts can thrive – and are surrounded by long grass, lush vegetation or damp ground for creatures to hide in without the risk of being mown over. Many garden ponds have a mix of native and non-native plants

▲ Broad-bodied chaser dragonfly in the author's garden.

▶ Frogs often breed in ponds in spring and their spawn is easy to spot before the tadpoles hatch.

around them but it's a good idea to stick largely to natives within the pond as they are likely to provide the greatest benefits to wildlife. Some non-native pond plants such as New Zealand pigmyweed (*Crassula helmsii*), floating pennywort (*Hydrocotyle ranunculoides*) and parrot's-feather (*Myriophyllum aquaticum*) have escaped out into the wider landscape causing serious problems. It seems hard to imagine, but plants escape ponds with ease on the feet of birds and in storm water, so a lot of the current wild invasions may well have been completely accidental.

The areas of shallow water in the sun around a pond are very biodiverse, but are prone to drying out when water levels fall in summer, which can expose plant roots, pond liner and planting baskets. You can manage how much water levels drop by ensuring some of your pond is in shade, having shelves at least 30 centimetres deep and covering the shallowest areas with shingle and stone to reduce evaporation and hide the pond liner. Having a puddled clay

pond liner rather than a butyl one, or lining the inside of your pond with shingle or subsoil and planting directly into that rather than using baskets, are also options. If possible, have a deep area to retain some water at all times. Deep areas that don't freeze in winter will benefit overwintering wildlife – at least 60 centimetres is needed but double that is better in northerly regions where prolonged freezing weather occurs. If you have space for a substantial deep area, this will allow you to maintain an attractive area of open water at all times, even when the vegetation around the edges fills out.

It is also ideal to design your pond so that it can be topped up with rainwater collected from a nearby roof. Try to avoid tap water as much as possible as the chlorine and nutrients can be harmful. Connecting a downpipe to your pond is ideal. You will be surprised how much a short summer shower can help refill your pond. Alternatively, you can collect as much rainwater as you can in a water butt and use

Native pond plants

◄ Flowering rush (*Butomus umbellatus*)

◄ Lesser spearwort (*Ranunculus flammula*)

◄ Bogbean (*Menyanthes trifoliata*)

◄ Water forget-me-not (*Myosotis scorpioides*)

◄ Purple loosestrife (*Lythrum salicaria*)

◄ Amphibious bistort (*Persicaria amphibia*)

◄ Flag iris (*Iris pseudacorus*)

◄ Water plantain (*Alisma plantago-aquatica*)

◄ Marsh marigold (*Caltha palustris*)

◄ Arrowhead (*Sagittaria sagittifolia*)

that to top up your pond when needed. If your downpipe is connected directly to the pond, you will need to have an overflow from the pond that allows water to soak away into your garden. Alternatively, your overflow can feed a bog garden planted with damp-loving plants or a 'rain garden' designed to hold water and release it slowly over time. Rain gardens are beautiful, dynamic features that are becoming increasingly popular in urban areas to prevent rainwater overwhelming our sewers and causing flooding. They need to be planted with specific species that can tolerate being underwater at times and dry at others, such as purple loosestrife, meadowsweet and *Iris sibirica*.

Planting your pond

There are lots of really attractive native plants suitable for planting in wildlife ponds. You'll need at least one oxygenator, such as hornwort (*Ceratophyllum demersum*) or water starwort (*Callitriche stagnalis*), which can just be placed in the pond and don't need to be rooted into anything. The rest will either need to be planted into pond baskets or hessian bags to avoid plastic, or directly into a layer of substrate inside the pond. Use pure grit or a mix of grit and subsoil (from excavating the pond) as your substrate for planting into, rather than topsoil or potting compost, as this helps keep nutrient levels low and deters algae. Specialist, low-nutrient aquatic soils and composts are available. Check the depth of water your pond plants will need above their crown – a 30 centimetre-deep shelf works for most marginals but native white water lilies (*Nymphaea alba*) like it deeper.

FACTORS THAT REDUCE GARDEN HABITAT

The main reasons why our gardens might not be able to support wildlife are a lack of the habitats described in this chapter, or disturbance to them, as well as the use of insecticides which either directly kills animals or removes their food source. However, there are a few other factors which many nature lovers might be surprised to find they are doing accidentally.

Night Lighting

The growing popularity of big security lights or permanent garden lighting is causing problems for some nocturnal animals, including bats and all the species they feed on (such as moths), which really need dark to hunt enough to survive. If you want to add atmosphere to your garden for entertaining on a summer evening,

▲ Lanterns for special occasions are nice but lots of light in a garden at night can disturb wildlife.

try candles in jars or lanterns. If you need to light a path or doorway, make sure lights can be switched off when not in use, and are illuminating the smallest areas required. They should not be any brighter than needed and it's best to keep beams directed downwards.

Is it okay to feed wildlife?

Providing water and food for hedgehogs, foxes and birds is popular and can bring you closer to these creatures but some perceive it as interfering with nature. There are some times when it is more useful than others – the depths of winter when everything is frozen, or during summer and autumn droughts. Take care to research the right food type and keep feeders and water supplies clean to avoid inadvertently spreading disease.

Cats

Many people view cats hunting birds and small mammals as part of the natural order of things, but domestic cats are descended from African wildcats, which obviously don't naturally occur in the British countryside. Consequently, our native birds and mammals have not evolved to live alongside them and their populations are impacted by the presence of so many pet cats hunting for much of the day and night. If you are the owner of a cat, consider putting a bell on its collar to make stalking prey a little harder – it doesn't need to hunt for food, after all! During the season when baby birds are fledging, you could also keep your cat in at night. It is probably best not to encourage birds into gardens patrolled by cats by erecting bird feeders or nestboxes but, if you do, be very careful to locate them where cats cannot reach.

Keeping Bees

Beekeeping has become very popular and there is something magical about keeping a colony of bees to collect nectar from flowers around your neighbourhood and convert it into honey. Honeybees have been in the UK for thousands of years and are excellent pollinators of crops so by keeping bees you may also be increasing fruit set. However, honeybees are not truly native creatures and so boosting their success is really not contributing to native biodiversity. They may also take resources from our native bees (who are just as good, if not better, pollinators) and can spread disease to them.

▶ Beehives can be useful in orchards for pollinating fruit but in some places honey bees may compete with wild bees for food.

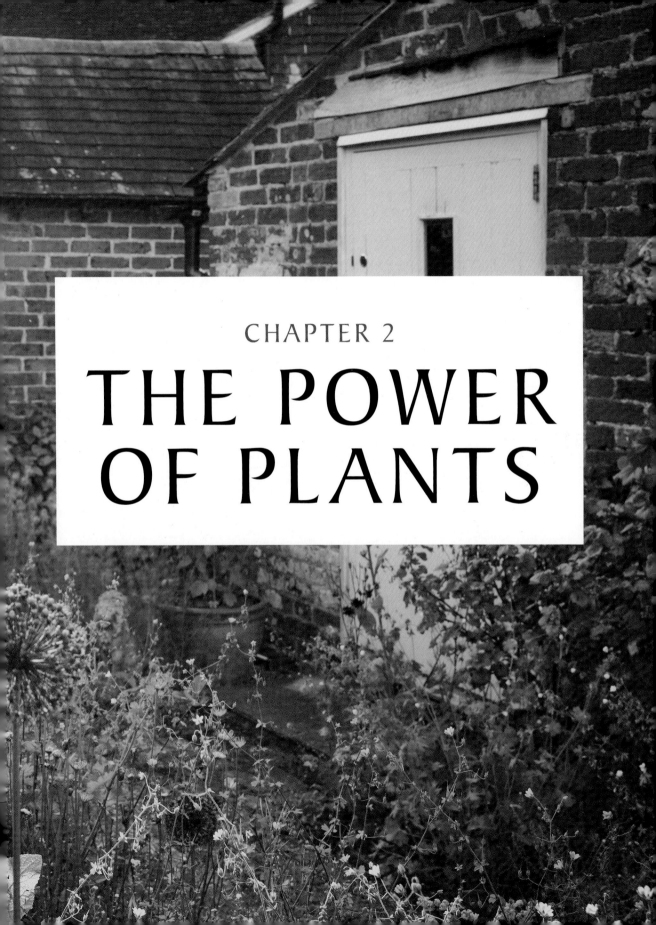

CHAPTER 2
THE POWER
OF PLANTS

THE POWER OF PLANTS

Plants form the basis of almost every garden. Research in Sheffield suggests the average domestic garden contains about 119 different species and that gardens cared for by keen gardeners have significantly more. It's clear that most gardeners enjoy plants, but do we understand their full value? Most of us choose which ones to grow based on their beauty – usually the dazzling colours and shapes of their flowers, but also their berries and leaves, architectural structure or autumn interest. Sometimes we factor in scent too, or a plant's edible or medicinal qualities. We tend to take for granted the other benefits they are providing for us, including capturing carbon, cleaning the air, muffling sound, providing shade, shelter or privacy as well as preventing erosion and absorbing water.

Equally important, and frequently overlooked, is the critical role garden plants can play in the lives of animals. The nectar that flowers offer to pollinating insects is one of the most talked-about benefits, but the picture is so much more complex than this: plants are able to provide food for numerous creatures at different stages in their life cycles in the form of pollen, leaf tissue, seeds, nuts, fruit and even rotting wood, as well as being places to hide, hibernate and breed.

▼ The borders at Packwood House in Warwickshire feature wonderful combinations of plants.

THE ORIGINS OF OUR GARDEN PLANTS

There are currently over 69,000 named garden plants listed in the RHS Plant Finder, the vast majority of which are varieties that have been selectively bred from a far smaller number of species. About 70 per cent of what we plant in our gardens derives from species that originated in other regions of the world. Some people find it very surprising to learn that a ubiquitous British garden plant such as lilac grows naturally in the rocky hills of the Balkans or that the ancestors of most cultivated roses were introduced from China.

Some very familiar non-native plants in Britain, such as apples and ground elder, have been established here since Roman times as they were introduced for food, medicine or other uses. However, the majority of our ornamental garden plants arrived later, from the 1500s onwards, when British traders were travelling the globe and explorers were deliberately seeking new botanical treasures to bring home. Many of our best-known garden plants were introduced in the 17th, 18th and 19th centuries, including rhododendrons, wisteria and hydrangeas from East Asia, dahlias from Central America, and agapanthus and red-hot pokers from southern Africa. New plants continue to be introduced, although strict rules about their collection and distribution govern the plant hunters of today.

▲ Red-hot pokers growing wild in Lesotho, Southern Africa.

The Value of Native Plants

Native plants are generally considered to be those that arrived in the UK without human intervention. Since very few plants survived the most recent ice age, most of the species we consider native will have arrived about 8,000–10,000 years ago when the ice had melted but the UK was still joined to the rest of Europe by a land bridge that enabled them to spread here. Conservationists argue that these are the plants which are of greatest value to wildlife as they have adapted alongside our native fauna to form complex, mutually dependent relationships.

Certainly, when it comes to insects and other invertebrates that feed on plants for all or some of their life, our native species tend to support the most. Birch, hawthorn, oak and willow are all famously good, each supporting 200 or more species. A close study of one native tree – the ash – showed 239 invertebrate species associated with it, 29 of which are likely to be dependent and not found on other plants. This exclusivity is not uncommon in herbivorous insects. It is thought that, as many plants evolved toxins in their tissues to ward off predators, certain insect species evolving alongside them overcame this and developed the ability to feed on them. The larvae of the striking cinnabar moth, for example, are adapted to eat ragwort which is toxic to other creatures. This is a brilliant adaptation, making the caterpillars and adult moths toxic to other predators, but it's devastating for the cinnabar moth when we humans begin to remove ragwort from the landscape to protect our livestock. Beautiful peacock and red admiral butterflies

▶ Hawthorn is a beautiful native tree which supports over 200 invertebrate species.

▼ Ragwort has been demonised by many but it's crucial food for the caterpillars of the cinnabar moth.

Buying native plants

It's great to grow your own native plants from seed collected within your local area. Never collect from protected species or significantly deplete any population – you only need a few seeds. Failing that, buy them from nurseries that specialise in UK native plants. Provenance can make a difference to a plant's genetic make-up and how well adapted it is to local conditions. Some native plants and seed for sale originate from cultivated forms with less genetic diversity or even from overseas populations, so use a well-established supplier who can prove the provenance.

have larvae that only eat nettles, or hops at a push. Specialisms or preferences are not only for creatures which eat leaves – the yellow loosestrife bee (*Macropis europaea*) seems only to collect the pollen it needs to feed its young and the floral oils it needs to line its nest from yellow loosestrife. These specialisms may explain why an RHS study, comparing the creatures present in a collection of native, near native and exotic gardens plants, found significantly more invertebrates present on the native plants.

With this in mind, it is good to know there are plenty of native plants that make great garden plants. For those of us who spend little time in wild places, these plants may actually be far less familiar and more interesting than some of the most common ornamentals. Being well suited to our soils and climate they are often hugely successful with minimum help.

Native trees and shrubs

◄ Silver birch (Betula pendula)
A very graceful, fast-growing tree. You need space to let this grow tall though, as it hates being pruned.

◄ Field maple (Acer campestre)
Flowers in spring and provides wonderful butter-yellow autumn colour. Becomes a large tree but can be pruned.

◄ Guelder rose (Viburnum opulus)
As beautiful as any ornamental shrub. The true native has lovely berries which the sterile hybrid doesn't.

◄ Dogwood (Cornus sanguinea)
This has deep red stem colour, subtler than the introduced varieties.

◄ Elder (Sambucus nigra)
Fast-growing and easy to prune, this is a great garden plant. The purple-leafed variety offers good wildlife value too.

Native Climbers

◄ Honeysuckle (Lonicera periclymenum)
A great plant for light shade, our true native form has creamy coloured flowers, far nicer than the pink hybrids from Holland.

◄ Ivy (Hedera helix)
An absolute must for a nature-friendly garden. Let it smother a shady fence and mature so that it flowers and bears berries.

◄ Hop (Humulus lupulus)
If the plain green leaves of this rampant climber don't excite you, there is a lime green form that has wildlife value too.

◄ Shrubby cinquefoil (Dasiphora fruticosa – formerly Potentilla fruticosa)
There are many cultivated varieties of this if you don't want the typical yellow flowers.

Native flowers

◀ **Foxglove (*Digitalis purpurea*)**
Tall, striking plant with impressive flowers in early summer; good in sun or shade.

◀ **Teasel (*Dipsacus fullonum*)**
A wonderful architectural plant for wild areas which can set seed rather too freely!

◀ **Purple loosestrife (*Lythrum salicaria*)**
Great in wet soil and pond margins but tolerant of drier spots too.

◀ **Valerian (*Valeriana officinalis*)**
Infinitely superior to the non-native red valerian, this is a very elegant and non-invasive plant, loved by insects.

◀ **Hemp agrimony (*Eupatorium cannabinum*)**
A bit of a thug so best to deadhead before it sets seed around the garden.

◀ **Field scabious (*Knautia arvensis*)**
Great in a meadow or sunny border with pale blue flowers carried on tall stems which are loved by bees.

◀ **Cow parsley (*Anthriscus sylvestris*)**
As good as many treasured umbels like *Ammi majus*.

◀ **Small scabious (*Scabiosa columbaria*)**
A short, neat scabious for a sunny border, which will flower for many months.

◀ **Musk mallow (*Malva moschata*)**
Shorter and bushier than common mallow (which is also native) with more attractive foliage.

◀ **Ox-eye daisy (*Leucanthemum vulgare*)**
A classic flower for a meadow or a very wild border.

Native flowers (continued)

◄ English bluebells (*Hyacinthoides non-scripta*)
This is a lovely spring-flowering bulb, but do make sure you get the elegant native ones, not their thuggish Spanish cousins.

◄ Cuckoo flower (*Cardamine pratensis*)
This elegant flower needs damp soil, so a wet meadow or pond edge is ideal. It's the favourite larval food plant for orange-tip butterflies.

◄ Red campion (*Silene dioica*)
Charming pink flowers which set seed readily so that new plants spring up here and there.

◄ Wood anemone (*Anemonoides nemorosa*)
One of the most delightful little spring flowers; usually found in woodland, it is best planted in drifts under shrubs.

◄ Wild carrot (*Daucus carota*)
A magnificent tall umbel, great for a meadow or wild area. Short-lived but will self-seed around.

◄ Solomon's seal (*Polygonatum multiflorum*)
A dramatic plant for shady areas. Try to get the true native plant and not a garden hybrid.

◄ Sweet woodruff (*Galium odoratum*).
Great for ground cover in shady areas or as an underplanting for shrubs in containers.

◄ Dog violet (*Viola riviniana*)
A useful low-growing evergreen for ground cover beneath roses and other shrubs.

◄ Betony (*Betonica officinalis*)
There's a fashionable variety of this known as 'Hummelo', but the true native species is just as lovely.

◄ Columbine (*Aquilegia vulgaris*)
A classic cottage-garden plant that looks great in most borders and will seed itself about. The true native is blue but there are many strains.

◀ Lily of the valley (*Convallaria majalis*)
If you find the right damp, shady place for this, it can form thick ground cover. The scented flowers make lovely posies.

◀ Meadow cranesbill (*Geranium pratense*)
As vibrant blue and long-flowering as many ornamental geraniums with lovely, dissected foliage.

◀ Great mullein (*Verbascum thapsus*)
Best for an open gravel garden and so popular with mullein moth larvae that it will end up looking a little ragged by the end of the season!

◀ Primrose (*Primula vulgaris*)
The true native primrose will grow almost anywhere. The pale yellow flowers are popular with long-tongued bumblebees.

◀ Nettle-leaved bellflower (*Campanula trachelium*)
Best for a shady border in a garden that isn't too damp or plagued with slugs and snails.

◀ Meadowsweet (*Filipendula ulmaria*)
Glorious fluffy, lightly scented flowers on tall stems which need a damp, wild corner of the garden.

◀ Greater knapweed (*Centaurea scabiosa*) and common knapweed (*Centaurea nigra*)
Great in sunny, well-drained borders or meadows where they attract insects. Leave seedheads for birds.

◀ Tuberous comfrey (*Symphytum tuberosum*)
Lovely nodding flowers appear in profusion over many months in spring; they are loved by bumblebees. Spreads quickly.

The Case for Non-Native Garden Plants

Many garden enthusiasts see things differently, arguing that non-native garden plants have not been studied well enough, that they offer huge benefits to nature and that many plant-eating insects have much broader tastes than have been recorded. They believe that it is the huge mix of plants of all kinds that make domestic gardens so special. Some even count the non-native plant species we introduce to gardens as adding to biodiversity in themselves.

Recent studies by the RHS have found that gardens are biodiverse because the wide range of plants with different structures and flowering times provides food almost all year round. Winter-flowering exotics are flagged

▼ Garden tiger moths are common in gardens as their caterpillars can eat the leaves of many plant species.

Leaf-cutting bees

There are seven species of leaf-cutting bees in the UK, which use sections of leaf to create cells within their nests. Some species favour certain native plants but many happily use garden plants, including roses, fuchsia, magnolia, azaleas, privet, lilac and even young bamboo. The notches they create never do serious damage to a plant and should always be welcomed as a sign of life.

as important, and likely to become more so if climate change brings increasingly mild winters, causing overwintering insects such as bumblebees to wake more frequently during winter or earlier in the year. These studies also pinpoint the density of cover and high number of evergreens that could lead to a greater abundance of some invertebrates.

Many of the creatures that get on best in our gardens are the generalists, such as the meadow spittle bug which sucks sap from almost any plant, and the garden tiger moth whose larvae seem to be able to eat a wide range of plants. There are also those that don't need living plant

tissue at all, but feed on rotting vegetation, faeces and other insects. Observational evidence in gardens also shows that some species thought to favour native hosts will happily use other plants. For example, ecologist Jennifer Owen witnessed mottled pug moths laying eggs on non-native garden plants weigela, peony and philadelphus, and brimstone butterfly larvae feeding on Japanese quince, when both are usually recorded as requiring a limited range of native plants. She also observed juniper shield bugs using other conifers besides juniper, and many gardeners have seen dramatic elephant hawk-moth caterpillars on fuchsia, a plant which originates from Chile, rather than its typical hosts, the willowherbs. Explanations for this include some species being

more generalist than first thought; some garden plants being closely related to native plants with very similar chemical properties, and some plants not having evolved off-putting toxins at all. There is evidence that the length of time a non-native plant species has been here and how widespread it is can be a factor in how well it supports wildlife. This might explain why common garden plants such as roses and apples attract a wide range of insects, many of them considered pests by those trying to grow perfect blooms or fruits!

▲ Studies have shown that a mix of native and non-native plants can boost biodiversity in our gardens. These borders at Nunnington Hall in North Yorkshire have natives like red campion and foxgloves growing among classic non-native garden plants.

A Happy Compromise

For those of us who wish to garden for wildlife, the evidence all points towards striking a compromise with what you plant. Choose a good mix of plants you love, ensuring they serve the functions you need in terms of beauty and structure, and will flower over a long period, providing nectar and pollen from early spring to late autumn, or even winter. It's fine if the majority of these are non-native garden plants, provided they are good for pollinators, but make sure a proportion are natives in the hope they will support a few specialist creatures who may be short of the food plants they need. You may wish to create a wilder area dedicated to these natives or distribute them through your borders. Some may need to be bought and planted, but with others it may just be a case of welcoming what springs up of its own accord.

Plants for Pollinators

Studies focussed on flying insects which feed on nectar and pollen in flowers show that plenty of non-native plants serve them very well. This is probably because nectar is largely the same sugar-rich liquid wherever it is found. While many plants have needed to develop toxic substances to protect their leaves from attack, and only certain insects have evolved to overcome this, the same has not happened with nectar because flowers generally wish to invite in all visitors.

Insects visiting flowers to feed on energy-rich nectar and also protein-rich pollen is not a one-way street. Plants have evolved to ensure insects do something magnificent for them in return. When flying insects land on flowers or burrow into them to feed, pollen from the male part of a flower is brushed onto their bodies where it can then be brushed off again on the female part of another flower. Flowers have evolved to make

this easy by holding their pollen on delicate stamens, which must be brushed past to get to the nectar, and then having a sticky female part that readily picks it up. Many even are designed to ensure the pollen is rubbed off on a different flower to the one it was collected from, in order to promote genetic diversity. Some common food crops, such as courgettes, have separate male and female flowers and so female flowers must be pollinated to produce the fruiting part we eat. Some, such as apples, must receive pollen from flowers of a different variety in order to set fruit. So, in areas where pollinators are declining because of the use of pesticides, there can be serious issues with crop yields. Gardens play a really big role in supporting all these pollinators because they are usually full of flowering plants. In urban areas or districts where farming is very intense and there are no longer any flowering meadows, hedgerows or verges, gardens may be the major source of nectar.

These days there is lots of information available about which plants will be visited by pollinating insects and many plant labels now include the RHS 'Plants for Pollinators' logo. Some of the most popular flowers are in the daisy family, as these are made up of many tiny flowers held together in an easy landing platform, with lots of readily accessible nectar. A good range of flowers in the garden is best though, as some species, such as the long-tongued garden bumblebee, have adapted to make use of deep, tubular blooms like foxglove, honeysuckle or snapdragon. The flowers to avoid are showy ones, bred to have many extra petals, meaning that there is often no nectar available, or that it's hard to access.

▶ Crocus are not native to Britain but are a great source of nectar and pollen for bumblebees in spring.

Garden shrubs for pollinators

◀ **Crab apple (*Malus* spp.)**
Most fruit trees that are laden with blossom in spring are popular with pollinators.

◀ **Oregon grape (*Mahonia* spp.)**
Great early flowering sources of nectar growing on a very tough shrub.

◀ **Californian lilac (*Ceanothus* spp.)**
Typically flowering for several weeks in spring and summer, these are really popular with bees and other pollinators.

◀ **Rosemary (*Salvia rosmarinus*)**
Useful for cooking but also tough, evergreen and loved by pollinators.

◀ **English lavender (*Lavandula angustifolia*)**
Perfect for pots or sunny borders, this is a magnet for pollinators.

Garden perennials for pollinators

◀ **Giant scabious (*Cephalaria gigantea*)**
A tall, statuesque perennial that is easy to grow with big and beautiful pincushion flowers.

◀ **Globe thistle (*Echinops* spp.)**
These are really striking but need a sunny situation. Flowerheads look stunning even in winter.

◀ **Round-headed garlic (*Allium sphaerocephalon*)**
All the alliums are good but this one is especially popular and beautiful.

◀ **Anise hyssop (*Agastache* spp.)**
Requires a sunny spot in free-draining soil. A huge hit with bees, butterflies, moths and more.

◄ **Lungwort (*Pulmonaria officinalis*)**
Great early source of nectar for bumblebees; grows in shade.

◄ **Marjoram (*Origanum vulgare*)**
A fabulous plant for the edge of a border, always teaming with life.

◄ **Sedum (*Hylotelephium spectabile*)**
This garden favourite offers nectar for many weeks in late summer and autumn.

◄ **Catmint (*Nepeta* spp.)**
Perfect for the front of a border, where it creates a dense mound, unless a cat can't resist stretching out on it!

Hoverflies

About 80 different species of bee and wasp visit our gardens but relatively few find the right conditions to breed there. Hoverflies, on the other hand, do well in gardens. There are 266 species in total, over 90 of which might be seen in gardens and at least 25 of which might breed. Many hoverflies mimic wasps, bees and bumblebees in the way they look, but differ in the way they fly – hovering apparently motionless, then darting away. Adults are usually around in July and August visiting flowers for pollen, nectar and honeydew. The larvae of different species feed on very different things, including rotting wood, plant tissues, fungi and ants' nests; some even live in water. Many of the species that thrive in gardens eat aphids, so should be made to feel very welcome!

CHOOSING PLANTS THAT WILL THRIVE IN YOUR GARDEN

Gardens filled with plants that are thriving are not only beautiful and good for wildlife but are better for soil health and carbon storage. Permanent, living plant roots feed organisms in the soil, which in turn feed plant roots, allowing plants to grow bigger, capture more carbon and release more sugars into the soil. Healthy plants growing like this need less feed and water and are less prone to pests and disease. Even regular mulching is not needed as the soil is healthy and weeding is minimised since established plants fill the space.

To achieve this, stick with shrubs and perennials rather than having half-empty beds, which get filled with annuals or tender plants in summer. Taking time to understand your soil and think about how much sun and rain reaches different parts of your garden before choosing new plants also really pays off. We need to move away from thinking of plants as objects for temporary display and understand them as intrinsic parts of the garden ecosystem, having specific needs and functioning above and below ground at all times of year.

The needs of a particular plant are generally dictated by where they come from; not just the region of the world but the habitat, be it woodland, meadow, mountainside or riverbank. An alpine phlox from a sunny, mountain slope, for example, is adapted to rooting in a thin layer of soil over rock so understandably suffers when planted in a rich, heavy garden soil, especially in the shade. Conversely, great

▶ Many National Trust gardens are a great place to see planting which is perfectly suited to the local site and soil conditions, as with this Mediterranean planting on a sunny hillside at Overbeck's in South Devon.

masterwort (*Astrantia major*) comes from damp lowland meadows in Central and Eastern Europe and wilts quickly if planted somewhere that bakes dry in summer. Of course, most gardeners are unlikely to research the natural habitat for each of the plants they buy, but there is good advice available about the amount of sun and soil conditions most plants need, and it is wise to follow it.

Understanding soil conditions

The main factors to understand are texture, structure, moisture levels and pH.

The texture of soil depends on how much sand or clay it contains. This will determine how much moisture it holds and is not something you can really change. Some people add grit to clay soils but this is not very sustainable; garden compost is better, but even this won't make a fundamental difference, and you will still need to choose plants suited to clay soils. You can check

the texture of soil by rolling some in a ball in your hand and seeing whether it holds together. Sandy soils won't roll up while clay soils can be rolled into a sausage shape. Most garden soils are somewhere in between.

Structure is about how the soil has been cared for, whether it's compacted from lots of walking over it so that water sits on the surface, or if it has plenty of air pockets to allow for drainage which makes life for plant roots easier. Structure can be improved over time with good soil management, including not walking on it in wet weather, mulching with compost and not leaving it bare (see page 125).

Soil moisture will depend on structure and texture, but also whether you're in sun or shade, whether there are any springs in your garden and how much rainfall you get. The key thing is that after heavy rainfall, water is able to drain away through the soil profile so that plant roots aren't

▲ Astrantia is a quick-growing plant for gardens with moist soils but will wilt quickly in sunny, sandy spots.

Plants for heavy clay soils in sun

Heavy soils which contain a lot of clay can bake dry in summer sun but then hold a lot of water in winter. Many sun-loving Mediterranean plants can't cope with this and will rot off over winter but there are some that thrive, so do your research if you have these conditions. Six of the most reliable include:

◀ **Elder (*Sambucus nigra*)**
A very easy shrub to grow which comes in purple and golden leafed varieties.

◀ **Goatsbeard (*Aruncus dioicus*)**
A statuesque and bushy perennial which flowers in early summer but has attractive foliage for many months.

◀ **Hydrangeas such as *Hydrangea paniculataa***
Most hydrangeas like moisture but will cope with baking dry in summer once they are well established.

◀ **Hardy geraniums like *Geranium* 'Johnson's Blue'**
There are many different geraniums, most of which will tolerate a heavy soil.

◀ **Japanese anemones (*Anemone x hybrida*)**
Very tough plants which add colour to the garden in late summer and autumn.

◀ **Red bistort (*Bistorta amplexicaulis*)**
An architectural perennial for late summer and autumn colour. There are varieties in pink, red and white.

saturated. If this isn't the case, you'll need to look for plants that like moist soils.

A soil's pH refers to how acid or alkaline it is, which depends on the area you are in, the soil texture and the underlying rock. There are tests you can easily buy at garden centres, or you can just look to see if your neighbours are successfully growing acid-loving plants, like rhododendrons and camellias. In the past gardeners would try to change their soil pH with additives so they could grow a wider range of plants but this is not necessary or sustainable.

Understanding Light Levels

Plants which are said to need a sunny site, probably need to be in a position that faces south or west, so that they get sun for about six hours of the day in summer. Plants for a lightly or partially shaded position are best facing east or west – or south if there is some shade from a tree or building. Plants for deep shade are the hardest to find but are needed for planting against north-facing walls and fences where the sun never reaches. Deep shade on a moist soil offers some opportunities for lush-leafed plants adapted to this. Deep shade on a soil made dry by tree roots or being in a rain shadow is a bigger challenge, but there are even plants that will tolerate this, including some ferns, cyclamen, geraniums and epimedium.

Experienced gardeners do sometimes deviate from the label recommendations with success. For example, a plant which likes sun is more likely to tolerate some shade if it's in a nice, warm, sheltered spot and the soil is never too wet, whereas a plant said to like partial shade may tolerate full sun if its roots are in a moisture-retentive soil. Plants growing alongside one another will also have an impact on the available light and water, which can influence their success for better or for worse.

Embracing shade

Many of our most popular garden plants are sun-lovers and so flower gardens have traditionally been situated in the sunniest areas possible. However, as much of the country sees increasingly frequent drought and water shortages, one simple solution is to create more borders in the shade. Partially shaded areas that receive morning or afternoon sun, but not the full heat of the middle of the day are ideal, and a vast range of plants are likely to thrive in them. The soil in these areas is likely to stay moist for longer, meaning far less irrigation is required.

Climate Change

Climate change is already affecting our lives, bringing extremes of wet and dry, cold and heat. Many gardeners will be aware of challenging conditions for growing plants and days of extreme heat where it's too hot to do anything but sit in the shade. Spring now seems to start a week or two earlier than it did a few decades ago, and all ten of the warmest years have occurred since 2003. Human-induced global warming is currently 1 degree Celsius above pre-industrial levels and is set to increase to 1.5 or more. The current thinking is that if this increase goes to above 2 degrees Celsius, then climate will overtake habitat destruction as the main reason for loss of animal and plant species. Bold initiatives to limit the worst effects of climate change are happening in the UK with organisations like the National Trust committing to becoming carbon neutral. However, we do need worldwide change and collaboration to avoid serious social, economic and environmental impacts globally.

One very tangible change affecting British gardens is that the range of plants we traditionally grow will be different. Most of the plants that thrive outside in UK gardens have been gathered from other similarly temperate regions of Europe, Asia and North America. A huge proportion originate from areas of China where the climate was similar to ours: cold and dry in winter but mild and moist through summer. As UK summers are becoming hotter

▼ Some of the magnificent rhododendrons at Sheringham Park in Norfolk are being propagated and relocated as they are unlikely to thrive in their current location in the future.

and drier, with prolonged droughts in the South East, and winters becoming milder and wetter, some of these plants are already struggling.

Selecting replacement plants is not straightforward. The long-term prediction for much of the UK is a Mediterranean climate but it will not be a smooth journey to get there. As we are already seeing, there will be cold springs, late frosts, high winds and unseasonal rains. Simply choosing more drought-tolerant plants from drier climates leaves us vulnerable to losing them in wet winters, conditions to which they are not adapted. There are increasing opportunities for growing less hardy plants from warmer climates such as yuccas, Chilean myrtle and schefflera, but spring frosts can be harsh, sudden and widespread, and are predicted to continue for many decades to come.

Our trees in particular are under threat. Many are experiencing great fluctuations in soil moisture levels around their roots, leading to stress, limb drop and root diseases. In the west, strong winds from a north-easterly direction have put pressure on established trees, while across the country milder winters are enabling new tree pests and diseases to flourish. When we plant a tree, we want it to live for several decades, even centuries, so it may need to withstand significant changes in the climate. For most woodland planting schemes, nature conservationists continue to invest mainly in natives of local origin, as these species are so crucial for the native wildlife and the whole woodland ecosystem. They recognise that some, such as beech, are becoming unsuitable for dry, southerly sites but hope many others will show resilience. Collectively we gardeners are probably

▶ If you live in a drought-prone area with free-draining soil, consider introducing more sun-loving, drought-tolerant plants in readiness for hotter, drier summers. The walled garden at Felbrigg in Norfolk has embraced this approach.

Tough garden trees for the future

◄ White willow (*Salix alba*)
Fast-growing, medium-sized shrub that can be coppiced; this will tolerate soil which fluctuates between very wet and dry. There are some nice ornamental varieties available.

◄ Scot's pine (*Pinus sylvestris*)
This native pine is drought-resistant and tolerates temporary waterlogging. It gets very big but you can remove the lower branches so that the canopy still casts some welcome shade. There are also dwarf forms.

◄ Downy birch (*Betula pubescens*)
A lovely tall, thin native tree with attractive bark, this is great for wildlife and also tolerant of soils that fluctuate between wet and dry.

◄ Pin oak (*Quercus palustris*)
Used a lot in landscaping projects, this American oak is quite fast-growing and tolerant of a wide range of conditions, including waterlogging and air pollution. Amazing autumn colour.

◄ Hawthorn (*Crataegus monogyna*)
A very tough little native tree with lovely blossom, which will grow in most soils and tolerate air pollution and wind.

◄ Crape myrtle (*Lagerstroemia indica*)
Native to China, this is suitable for sheltered, sunny city gardens where frosts don't occur. Very drought tolerant and attractive.

best hedging our bets and taking a mixture of approaches, be it choosing tough natives, trying new varieties of well-known species, selected to be more drought tolerant or disease resistant, or experimenting with altogether different species originating from less temperate climates. Some horticulturalists argue that in the future non-native tree species may provide resources for birds and invertebrates which come to the UK as a result of climate change. However, predicting which animals will change their natural ranges and what they will need is complicated and something few gardeners would be able to plan for.

Invasive Plants

Many of the plants introduced into the UK from elsewhere have thrived here, and now grow freely outside gardens. Mexican fleabane (*Erigeron karvinskianus*), for example, can often be seen poking out of cracks in a pavement while buddleia will quickly colonise a brownfield site. In urban areas this may bring some additional colour and provide nectar and pollen for flying insects. Some even argue the resilience of these

▲ Crocosmia can be a lovely garden plant, especially if you choose named garden varieties, but never allow it to spread into the countryside.

plants in the face of disturbance and heat may make them increasingly useful in the future.

However, for those interested in protecting native biodiversity it is concerning that the latest version of the Plant Atlas shows that of the 3,500 species growing wild in the UK, almost half are now non-natives and that a small number of these have become invasive. Non-native plants are classed as invasive when they spread quickly and are hard to remove and so begin to dominate part of our landscape, pushing native plants out of the way and changing the habitat. One of the most famous examples is *Rhododendron ponticum*, a beautiful shrub first recorded in the UK in 1763, which now clothes vast areas of the South West, shading out all beneath it and altering the soil. Another is Japanese knotweed (*Reynoutria japonica*), introduced from Japan in 1849, which is now such a problem that people selling properties must declare if it is present; when it is dug out the resulting vegetation is classed as controlled waste. Himalayan balsam (*Impatiens glandulifera*), a relative of the harmless busy lizzie, was introduced in 1839 and is equally problematic, moving by seed through watercourses and lining our riverbanks so that little else can grow. There are many other examples too which have the status of invasive plants, making it an offence to allow them to grow in the wild. Some of these are so well established and familiar and it might surprise people to know they are covered by law. These include montbretia (*Crocosmia × crocosmiiflora*), many cotoneasters, *Gunnera manicata* and *G. tinctoria*, Japanese rose (*Rosa rugosa*) and Japanese honeysuckle (*Lonicera japonica*). A number of water plants are also included, some of which are illegal to sell. Invasive water plants

can be moved from our garden ponds as seed or fragments of root by birds and amphibians and get into watercourses where they can then spread quickly and destroy important habitats. Managing invasives on water is also really tricky and often involves pesticides. That's why it is wise to stock your pond with mostly native plants (see page 48) and to steer clear of aquatic plant suppliers who deal in novel species.

Plants which have been identified as invasive and controlled by law are those which are already causing major problems and costing the people who manage land (including the National Trust) vast sums to control. But there are many other plants in our gardens with invasive tendencies, or plants which could become invasive in the future when temperatures rise further. Anyone who has tried to clear an area of Russian vine (*Fallopia baldschuanica*), snowberry (*Symphoricarpos albus*) or a spreading bamboo will be horrified to know they are all available for sale. Then there is the brilliant green hedging plant *Griselinia* that spreads and seeds like wildfire in mild areas, or fashionable pheasant grass (*Anemanthele lessoniana*) which, once introduced to a garden, seems to spring up everywhere. So, it's worth thinking very responsibly about what you plant, especially if your garden borders an area of special countryside. We need to be a bit more forward-thinking about this subject than our forefathers were. After all, we are only custodians of our gardens and when we pass them on, many of the plants we leave behind will outlive us by centuries. For more advice about how to keep an eye on thuggish plants see page 116.

◄ One to watch. The beautiful chocolate vine *Akebia quinata* is a major problem in New Zealand and the USA. It's too cold in the UK for it to set seed and spread but that could change in the future.

Please pay at the
Honesty Box the
plant sale area

SUSTAINABLY
ORGANICALLY
GROWN FRESH
GARDEN
PRODUCE

CHAPTER 3

BUYING RESPONSIBLY

BUYING RESPONSIBLY

Gardening is a huge industry in the UK, with householders spending over £6 billion on plants, compost and other gardening materials annually. Many of those purchases bring a lot of pleasure to people and encourage them to spend time outside, and some also support innovative and sustainable businesses. Sadly however, like so many other industries, a lot of the plants and materials available to buy are not sustainably produced or intended to last, and there is a huge amount of waste created.

Gardeners who choose to seek out ethically made, long-lasting products in shops and online can have a real impact on what is available for sale. Use your purchasing power and don't be afraid to ask questions at your local garden centre about where the plants and materials have come from. Try to plan your shopping so that you only buy what you really need and resist impulse buys. There are usually many things we can manage without or find second-hand, and others we could perhaps pay a little more for to ensure they stand the test of time and are made with the best possible standards of production.

▲ Many National Trust gardens have sales areas where they stock plants grown peat free by the garden team or trusted suppliers.

PLANT SHOPPING

One of the biggest changes in recent years is how many plants we routinely buy and how few we raise ourselves. Many are bought on impulse, often in large containers, in full flower. They look so appealing and colourful that they can be very hard to resist, but it's worth being aware that they have quite a big environmental footprint, as they will have taken a lot of water, fertiliser and compost to produce, need big plastic pots and may even have been grown abroad. They are often growing in composts containing peat (a precious natural resource that has been extracted from wetlands) and may have been sprayed with a number of pesticides.

Many of these plants are quite expensive and don't always establish well, especially in dry weather. A lot of the varieties are selected for how attractive they look in the pots rather than how good they'll be in the garden, and a vast number are tender or annual plants that will die in winter and need to be replaced the following year. Classic plants to resist are soft, slug-prone delphiniums in full flower, tender chrysanthemums and short-lived ranunculus. If you plant these in summer you may get a splash of instant colour, but once the flowers are gone the plant is unlikely to put down roots, get through winter and reappear. Fortunately, there are far more sustainable ways to buy plants which are generally more affordable and less likely to lead to disappointment.

Plants That Will Last

Annual bedding plants are appealing because of their bright and plentiful flowers but they need a lot of feed, water and deadheading and even then only last one season. If you want to spend your money more wisely, choose shrubs and hardy perennials that you'll only have to buy once. Try

to think beyond simply the flowers – these will usually only last a few weeks – but there is so much more to a plant than that. As explained on page 68, some plants will be far better suited to the site you have than others, so will establish well and be less likely to need replacing; do read plant labels carefully. It's wise to be realistic

Long-lived plants for container displays

Even containers can be planted with shrubs and perennials rather than bedding plants to reduce how often you need to replace them. Lavender, rosemary, agapanthus, cistus, hostas, erigeron and catmint all grow really well in pots, and most of them have flowers that are attractive to pollinating insects. You can put small bulbs like crocus and Siberian squill (*Scilla siberica*) under them for a bit of spring interest. Use the biggest container possible and choose a loam-based compost (one that contains soil, often called John Innes) to hold water and nutrients.

about the space you have available and the size
the plant will grow to, as well as thinking about
the overall shape it will have in the garden and
the qualities of the leaves. Flowering time is
important too, as you'll need to have plants that
will be in flower at different times of the year,
not all at once in summer.

Try to research the plants you need online
or in books before going plant shopping and
don't expect to find everything you need in
your local garden centre. When you are plant
shopping, take along a knowledgeable friend,
ask questions of the staff or look plants up on
your smartphone for more information. Try to
resist impulse buys at supermarkets where there
is no one around to advise. Shopping at smaller
nurseries that grow their own plants can be the
most rewarding experience. These nurseries often
specialise in particular species and have expert
staff who can advise you on what the plants need
in order to thrive.

When you buy perennials, try to buy them
as small as possible because small plants tend to
establish better and require less water. It's also
wise to buy them in spring or autumn and plant
them when the soil is moist. The smaller size
and time of year may mean that they are not in
flower, which might make them less appealing,
but this is actually better for their establishment.
With roses, hedging plants and many deciduous
shrubs, buying online in autumn and winter
means you can buy 'bareroot' and they'll be
lifted from the ground when dormant and sent
out without pots or compost. This is a very
sustainable way to source plants and they usually
establish well. Some perennials are available this

▶ Once introduced to a garden, perennials such
as these lupins, cornflowers and ornamental chervil
will last forever.

way too. Planting bareroot plants means you can see the roots and splay them out carefully in the planting hole, whereas roots in a container can become pot bound.

A plant type that has gained immense popularity in recent years is the tulip. Whereas our grandparents used to grow tough, Darwin-type tulips, which lasted for years in beds and borders, we tend to grow very fancy varieties in pots which last only one or two seasons. These are produced in Holland in very intensive ways that are not great for the soil. If you can't live without tulips, look for varieties known to be more perennial. Alternatively, choose completely perennial bulbs like narcissus, scillas, muscari and alliums, which you shouldn't have to replace very often, if at all. Many of these have more value for wildlife too.

Choosing Peat Free and British Grown

One of the advantages of shopping around for your plants is that you can also search out those that have been grown peat free, preferably in the UK. By doing this you will usually be supporting smaller businesses, ideally local to you.

Peat is an amazing spongy kind of soil that has formed over thousands of years in wetlands. Because it can hold water really well, and has a fine, even consistency it has been used for several decades to grow plants in. However, harvesting it involves destroying precious wetland habitats and releasing a lot of stored carbon into the atmosphere, so it's high time we all stopped using it. There are now plenty of composts available that don't contain peat, and plants for

THESE PLANTS ARE GROWN HERE BY OUR GARDEN TEAM

sale which have been grown without peat. If you can't find what you need, do tell your garden centre or supermarket that you want peat-free plants. Unless gardeners show that we don't want to be responsible for the destruction of habitat, the industry won't have an incentive to become fully peat free.

Not only does the global trade in plants have a high carbon footprint, it has also led to the introduction of unwanted insects and plant diseases that threaten our gardens, woodlands and even our food security. For example, a disease called ash dieback was introduced with imported ash trees, and is now set to wipe out 60–90 per cent of our native ash trees. Numerous other pathogens pose an even greater threat, many of them capable of arriving here on a garden plant such as lavender or maple. The government have put controls in place and undertake inspections of some consignments, but it is impossible for them to check everything, so we can play our part by buying British-grown and showing that it matters to us as consumers. With support and positive action, let us hope British horticulture will one day be able to supply all our needs.

The easiest plants to find British-grown are perennials from specialist nurseries, hedging plants and fruit trees. The hardest will be evergreens, topiary and large shrubs and trees, which are commonly imported, so do think carefully about whether you really need these and make sure they look healthy.

GROWING YOUR OWN PLANTS

Probably the most sustainable way of acquiring a new plant for your garden is being given a cutting or division from a friend's garden. The travel miles will be few, there'll be no need for a new pot and it might even have been something they were throwing away because it was doing so well they had more than they needed! You can also grow your own plants from seed. Even if you buy the seed rather than collect it, it'll have a low carbon footprint since it is small and light to transport and needs minimal packaging.

Divisions

Many hardy perennial plants are very easy to divide so that you can turn one plant into several more. These include lungwort, hardy geraniums, astrantia, iris, epimedium and sedums. Some large, old clumps even benefit from being lifted, split and having sections put back in the ground. Maybe you can help a friend do this in return for some of their spare plants?

◀ Buying locally grown plants is a sustainable option.

▶ Hostas can be divided in spring or autumn by digging them up and slicing the rootball into sections.

There are lots of books and videos available to show you how best to divide particular plants. The key is to go for plants with multiple growing points, not ones with stems that all originate from the same point in the ground. For success, you'll just have to ensure there is plenty of root and some strong growing points on each of the sections you replant. You can lift the whole clump and split it up by hand or with tools. Alternatively, if you don't need to disturb the main plant, you can try just slicing a bit off one edge. Mid-autumn is the best time for most plants, just as they are beginning to die back, but the soil is still warm enough for roots to recover quickly from the disturbance.

Cuttings

If you see a shrub you like in a friend's garden, the chances are it will be growing from one main point and therefore can't be split apart and propagated by division. Instead, the best way is to take a cutting from a healthy shoot and try to persuade it to produce roots. This is nowhere near as easy as taking divisions, but very satisfying indeed. Shrubs which root easily from cuttings include sage, rosemary and potentilla. Other plants you might not think of as shrubs,

▲ Lavender can be propagated by taking stem cuttings in summer.

but which grow from one point include everlasting wallflowers and penstemon, and these are super-easy to grow from cuttings.

There is a lot of advice online about which species should be propagated as 'hardwood', 'semi-ripe' or 'softwood' cuttings. This simply refers to the age and flexibility of the piece of stem you try to root. The most important thing is to ensure your cutting has a nice clean cut just below a leaf or bud and that you keep it humid while it roots. The easiest way to do this is to push it down into a small pot filled with moist potting compost, water it and then cover with an upside-down jam jar to act as a mini greenhouse. Then put it in light shade and don't water it again for at least two weeks (as it doesn't have any roots to take up the water and you don't want it to rot.) After about 4–6 weeks you'll be able to look through the hole under the pot or gently tug the cutting to see if it's made roots. It's always wise to do a few cuttings as it is normal for only half to succeed. Most of the hardy shrubs recommended here can be taken as cuttings in July, and should have rooted by the time the cold weather comes, so this is all possible without a greenhouse. More tender plants such as pelargoniums, and houseplants like tradescantia, are also easy to propagate from cuttings but you'll need a warm, light windowsill for success.

Seed

You can grow almost all plants from seed, including trees, shrubs and perennials, but some of them may need a little persuasion to germinate and you'll have to wait for them to reach flowering size. The easiest plants to grow from seed are hardy annuals and biennials. These can be sown in pots or directly into the ground in spring and will flower that summer or the following summer. Once introduced into your garden, many will set seed and spring up again of their own accord, or you can collect the seed and resow it where you want it.

Propagating climbers

Many climbers can be propagated by cuttings but some will naturally send out roots when they touch the ground. You can pin shoots down to the ground to encourage them to do this or find sections that already have rooted, and cut them off to create a new plant. Among the easiest ones are honeysuckle, loganberry, akebia, ivy and climbing hydrangea (pictured).

Easy Plants to Grow from Seed

◀ Common marigold (*Calendula officinalis*) Popular with bees and many other invertebrates, this has big seeds that are easy to collect for sowing again the following year.

◀ Foxglove (*Digitalis purpurea*) Our native foxglove is a magnificent biennial; seeds germinate and grow one year then flower the next, but once you have a population established you'll have a ready supply of new plants to move where you want them.

◀ Love-in-a-mist (*Nigella damascena*) This beautiful flower is followed by a magnificent seedhead which disperses lots of tiny seeds that will mean new plants spring up all over your garden.

◀ Honesty (*Lunaria annua*) Attractive flowers are followed by elegant seedheads which scatter their seed gently around the garden. Leaves support the larvae of orange-tip butterflies.

◀ Forget-me-not (*Myosotis sylvatica*) This is biennial but, like love-in-a-mist, once you have it, you'll have it forever, and may even need to weed some seedlings out each autumn.

◀ Teasel (*Dipsacus fullonum*) Flowers are popular with insects but it's the seedheads which are the real wow, lasting for many months. Can rather take over, so be prepared to weed out surplus seedlings.

CHOOSING SUSTAINABLE MATERIALS

In addition to plants, there are many other gardening-related products that we routinely buy including composts, aggregates, furniture, tools and all those little sundries. Their association with gardening makes them seem harmless, but everything has an impact on the planet in its production and transport, so it's worth stopping to consider what you really need and then choosing wisely.

Most garden sheds are stuffed full of tools no one uses. If you're starting out and want to stock up, ask around or look at online marketplaces and reclamation yards for what's going spare. Good, old, solid garden forks, spades, rakes, shears and hoes from these places are often very affordable and usually better made and longer lasting that what is available new. Good-quality steel can usually be sharpened by hand or by a blacksmith if needed, meaning tools last forever.

▼ Long-lasting tools in the gardener's storeroom at The Weir in Herefordshire.

COMPOSTS AND MULCHES

The term compost is used very freely in gardening and refers to a number of different things. Unfortunately, this is not always clear to gardeners who have been sold multi-purpose composts for use almost everywhere, when in fact quite different products are needed for potting plants compared to what's best for spreading onto soil or into planting holes.

The most sustainable kind of compost is the one you make yourself in your own garden by rotting down garden waste and, ideally, veg peelings from the kitchen. For more advice on how to do this see page 140. This has no transport miles attached to it and is full of nutrients so it's ideal for spreading on the soil as a mulch, or adding to planting holes. If it's very well-rotted it can also be sieved and mixed with other ingredients, such as sharp sand, sieved soil (molehill soil is ideal) and composted leaves, to make your own potting compost.

The compost you buy in bags is usually called all-purpose or multi-purpose compost but there are also some blends specifically for seed sowing or other purposes. These days this is made from a number of different ingredients, but for a long time the main constituent was peat, which we now know to be highly unsustainable. Peat-free composts are usually clearly labelled and are made from mixes of composted green waste, composted wood or bark, sometimes wool or bracken, soil and coconut fibre (known as coir). They are expensive to make and some of their

ingredients may have travelled great distances, so it's important to only use these for potting plants and never for spreading on beds. You can also make them go further by mixing them, if possible, with your garden soil when potting into large containers.

If you need a product for mulching beds and borders and haven't got enough of your own homemade garden compost, there are other products you can buy. Professional gardeners call these soil improvers and they include well-rotted manure, composted green waste and mushroom compost (left over from commercial mushroom growing). The most sustainable choice will be the one that has been produced nearest to you. None are perfect and they may all have contaminants, be it animal-wormers in manure, microplastics and weedkillers in green waste, or the excess lime in mushroom compost. So do stop and think before buying. It may help to know that, contrary to traditional wisdom, not all garden beds require regular mulching and it's best to save this for where the nutrients are really needed. For more advice on this see page 140. If you do need a large quantity of one of these products, try to get a loose load rather than buying it packaged in small, thick plastic sacks, which are very hard to recycle.

◀ Veg peelings can be added to your compost heap.

▲ Mulching along the base of newly planted hedges in autumn can help them establish well.

Aggregates

Other bagged materials for sale at the garden centre include grit, gravel and sand. While these are naturally derived products, it's worth remembering they are fragments of rock which formed over millions of years and are not renewable. Their mining causes disruption to landscapes and habitats, and fossil fuels will have been used in their extraction and transport. With this in mind, try to think if you really need the material before buying it – a small amount of sharp sand or grit to make a very free-draining compost for a long-lived plant is probably not going to do much harm, while endlessly digging it into a border of clay soil is a waste. Ask questions of your suppliers too – smooth pebbles, rounded gravel and soft sand extracted from riverbeds is likely to be more harmful to habitats than the angular materials extracted from quarries. If you really want to grow plants in the ground through a substantial layer of aggregate, look for recycled materials such as crushed brick, supplied as locally as possible.

Hard-landscaping

If you're redesigning your garden and planning to create new paths, seating areas, benches or other fixed items, try to think creatively about a solution and not leap to the traditional answer. On page 36 there are ideas about materials that will also provide habitat for wildlife. If possible, try to make use of materials that are already

◀ Garden paths can be created with a wide range of materials, including reclaimed stone, concrete slabs or brick and gravel – or any mixture of these, as seen here at Gunby Hall in Lincolnshire.

there or seek out reclaimed and recycled items. You might be surprised by what amazing stone, bricks or reclaimed slabs are available locally if you look at online marketplaces or visit reclamation yards. If someone is doing your paving for you, warn them you plan to use items like these and build in time to collect them. Hopefully they will support your ambition.

If you do need to buy new products, it can be difficult to work out which are the most or least sustainable and what standards to expect from

suppliers, so don't be afraid to ask questions. Some are beginning to include carbon emissions per square metre for their products, which is really helpful for consumers choosing between items made of clay, concrete, porcelain, local

Permeable surfaces

Another factor to consider with paving is permeability, so that water can be absorbed and doesn't flow off, adding to pressure on sewers. This is especially important in areas where there are a lot of hard surfaces. It's possible to design seating areas and even parking bays to be permeable so they can absorb water into the ground beneath.

stone or imported stone. In addition to carbon footprint, it's good to consider the ethics of certain purchases from overseas. Research has shown that the mining of highly popular, affordable materials such as Indian sandstone pavers may involve people (including children) working in terrible conditions, and suppliers need to be confident they are not supporting such exploitation.

Wood can be a very sustainable building material and decking is a lower-impact solution for a sunny spot than levelling and paving an area. However, the sustainability of wood varies massively depending on where it is sourced. Whenever you're buying new timber or ready-made wooden items, such as fence panels, trellis, sheds or benches, try to get UK-grown wood, certified to FSC or PEFC standards to be sure your garden is not playing a part in deforestation elsewhere. With wood products you already own, do look after them well to ensure longevity. Bringing in wooden garden furniture over the winter is important. If you can't do this, at least keep it somewhere dry and consider oiling it. If it still rots, it might be best to replace it with reclaimed metal or recycled plastic furniture.

◄ Even your garden furniture can be made with recycled materials, like this lovely bench at Chirk Castle, Wrexham, carved from a fallen tree.

Green roofs and walls

Green walls and roofs are often proposed as environmental solutions to buildings in gardens. Green roofs do have benefits in private gardens, mainly providing additional opportunities for plant species to grow and a very attractive view for neighbours who can see your roof. Green walls however are a bit of a gimmick, requiring a lot of infrastructure and maintenance. Nature has already invented a solution for greening-up a vertical surface – the climber!

REDUCING WATER USE, FOSSIL FUELS AND PLASTICS

Traditional gardening, which places neatness and productivity above all things, can lead to very high water use as well as dependence on fossil fuels for machinery and heating greenhouses. The good news is that for most domestic gardeners, it's possible to significantly reduce this consumption and still have a wonderful garden.

Water

The water which comes out of our taps has been collected, treated so that it is fit for human consumption and transported around a complex pipe network. Using this water on plants is wasteful, putting strain on water supplies in dry spells when they can least cope with it. Being dependent on tap water also leaves gardeners vulnerable in a hosepipe ban, plus it's not the ideal type of water for our plants as some may be sensitive to the lime, sodium or chorine it contains. What plants like best is rainwater, so the more of that you can capture the better. Small water butts collecting from the roofs of sheds and greenhouses are easy to install and often give you water sources in useful locations around the garden. However, these butts tend to fill quickly, overflowing all winter, and then empty quickly when you start using them in summer. For more effective water storage, consider connecting a really large butt or series of butts to a downpipe from your house roof. Not only will this store more water that will last for longer, but also, because of the larger surface area of the roof, it will refill quickly after a rain shower in summer, which is when you need it. Use a diverter so that when the butt is full it will revert to draining down into the drains, away from your house. Many people keep the majority of their containerised plants on terraces

close to the house so a water butt there will be convenient, but if you can also rig up a way of moving water to your veg garden, so much the better.

In addition to storing water, it's always worth reducing how much water you need during those really long, dry spells and also to save you

the time and stress of watering on hot summer days or worrying about plants when you're away from home. Ways to save water include choosing plants that are drought tolerant, reducing the amount of bare soil you have in the garden and the number of plants you keep in containers. Pots tend to need daily watering in hot weather whereas plants in the ground are more likely to cope between rain showers. It's also important to water wisely. If you need to water newly planted or struggling plants, go for a thorough water

▲ A water butt connected to a shed, greenhouse, garage or house roof will collect rainwater for use when you need it.

Water-saving containers

If you only have a small patio or balcony, most of your gardening might be in containers and these can be very thirsty in summer, requiring daily irrigation. Tips for success while saving water include using the biggest containers you can, moving them into shade during droughts and using a loam-based compost. Small containers which dry out are best reserved only for cacti and succulents and it's wise to avoid old-fashioned hanging baskets altogether. Consider saving water from baths or washing up to water plants and choose species such as silverbush (*Convolvulus cneorum*) and small hebes which aren't too thirsty.

infrequently and do it in the evening so plant roots are moist and cool all night. Never bother watering your lawn, unless it's recently been sown or laid as turf. It may look a bit parched but it'll always recover.

Greenhouse Heating

Many keen gardeners have a greenhouse in which to start plants early, overwinter more tender plants and grow heat-loving crops like tomatoes in summer. But this is quite a luxury and absolutely not necessary in a typical, small nature-friendly garden.

If you do have a greenhouse, it's best for the environment and your heating bills if you don't heat it. Heating structures made of glass, even just enough to keep them frost free, is expensive and uses a lot of energy. If you want to grow

▶ Even without heating, greenhouses can provide a bit of protection for plants in cold weather.

plants from seeds that need heat to help them germinate, start them off on a sunny windowsill, and move them outside in April or May once the temperature is high enough for the seedlings to cope. If you want to grow plants that aren't fully hardy, many will overwinter outside if they are moved into a sheltered place such as up against a house wall. If you absolutely must have a heated greenhouse, heat the smallest area possible and insulate it to conserve heat. Look for the most efficient electric heater you can find and consider switching to a green energy supplier if you haven't already.

Power Tools

In recent years mechanised tools have become increasingly popular – leaf blowers instead of rakes; hedge-trimmers instead of shears; strimmers instead of edging shears. If you only have a small amount of hedging or lawn, try sticking with the traditional method. For the smallest lawns there are even push-along lawnmowers. Doing things by hand where you can is good exercise, much quieter and uses less of the Earth's resources. Where you do need mechanised kit, look at plug-in or battery-

powered rather than petrol. Electric kit is generally quieter, lighter and less polluting and, if your electricity is from a green energy supplier, far more sustainable. If you have a big garden and require lots of equipment, try to invest in items that use the same battery as lithium batteries are expensive and their production has a high environmental cost.

Plastics

Plastics are everywhere in horticulture, just as in other aspects of our lives. In fact, the popularity of artificial plastic plants is even on the rise, and fake plastic grass can be seen in many gardens! Fortunately, awareness about plastic waste is increasing and many of us now know that just being aware of recyclable plastic and putting it out with our recycling isn't enough. A huge amount of energy has gone into making any plastic item, more will go into recycling it and lots of recyclable plastics get thrown away due to lack of facilities and contamination. We also know that plastics left to degrade in the environment break down into microplastics that pollute the soil and sea and find their way into the food chain.

Plant pots are one of the biggest problems. It's useful to have a few in the garden, especially the smaller ones for sowing seed, but most of us end up with far too many. Ways to stop that happening include growing more of your own plants, buying bareroot plants where possible, buying smaller plants in smaller pots or looking for plants sold in biodegradable pots. If you do buy plants in pots, look for coloured rather than black plastic pots – as it is more likely these can be recycled – or for ones made of recycled

▲ Making your own plant labels is one way of cutting down on plastics. Use lolly sticks or strips of plastic yoghurt pots. At Nunnington Hall in North Yorkshire, gardeners cut lengths of hazel for a really attractive effect in the veg garden.

plastic. Ask at your local garden centres or nursery if you can return pots. Find out if they plan to reuse them or at least know for certain that they will be recycled.

There are lots of other plastics too. Some are materials that hopefully we will use over and over again, like a piece of mesh for netting crops, but many are single use such as plant labels, the containers of liquid feed and strimmer wire. There are also hidden plastics which it pays to be aware of, including the fine mesh within rolls of turf and the microplastics in fertiliser pellets and synthetic water gels.

◄ Where you do need mechanised kit, look at plug-in or battery-powered rather than petrol.

CUTTING OUT GARDEN CHEMICALS

There is an arsenal of insecticides, fungicides, weedkillers, slug pellets, cleaning products and man-made fertilisers available to gardeners in the UK. Most of them are manufactured with high energy costs, packaged in plastic and transported long distances; some will be tested on animals. Few of them work as instantly as hoped by gardeners and many are accidentally misused so that excess runs into watercourses or harms unintended species. While this industry is regulated, environmentalists argue that the long-term impacts of these products on the environment and human health are not fully understood.

So, when you're drawn to a benign-sounding product such as 'lawn weed and feed', have a read of the ingredients and think about what your lawn really needs. Raking excess moss and dead grass from the surface by hand will give far better results that applying a chemical which will kill every other plant species besides the grass, leaving dead material that will still need raking out, and potentially harm soil organisms. Similarly, why reach for a rose spray, containing a mix of toxic insecticides and fungicides, when in fact all it probably needs is a good prune and thick mulch in winter?

Insecticides

Bug sprays are alarmingly easy to buy and spritzing our garden plants with poisons has become normal. Insecticides are usually either made of soaps and oils intended to suffocate insects, or are made of longer-lasting substances absorbed by a plant and intended to poison an insect when it bites into the foliage. Application instructions usually advise ensuring you know what problem you are trying to target, and not spraying a plant when it is in flower, in order to avoid harming pollinating insects. But how many gardeners are able to precisely identify the insect they wish to eliminate, understand it's life cycle enough to know when treatment will be effective and are aware of all the benign species which might also be on the plant and get hurt? For these reasons, some countries are banning the use of these products by amateur gardeners who have not received training.

Less than one per cent of the insects in Britain do any damage to garden plants. Jennifer Owen's famous study of her garden in Leicester found 50 species of moth breeding, yet she found almost

◀ Many birds including blue tits need to feed their young exclusively on protein-rich insects.

▶ The garden at Nunnington Hall in North Yorkshire is run on organic principles. Sometimes visitors report sightings of aphids on roses to the Head Gardener, but he never takes action as he knows the aphids cause minimal damage to the roses, and that blue tits in the garden will be hatching around the same time and the fledglings will work acrobatically through the roses to remove them.

no caterpillar damage which actually affected the health of her plants. Even caterpillars that cause small amounts of damage to our plants, such as winter moth on apples, shouldn't be poisoned as they are an important, nutrient-rich food source for the young of many breeding birds, such as great tits and blue tits. We can spare ourselves a lot of unnecessary worry and contamination of our environment if we learn to live alongside these creatures. We also need to remember that while biodiversity (the mix of species) is important, biomass (the overall volume of living things) is critical too. The last few decades have seen a marked impact on the abundance of even common creatures that are food for other invertebrates, birds, bats and small mammals. Prolific but persecuted species, such as aphids, ants, mosquitoes and flies, are all really important for making up this insect biomass.

Slug pellets

For the last few decades it has been common practice for gardeners to scatter slug pellets made of metaldehyde around their plants to attract slugs and snails and poison them. After mounting evidence that these were also toxic to birds and mammals (including pets), and the finding of metaldehyde in water bodies, they have now been removed from market. Alternatives using less toxic chemicals like ferric (iron) phosphate are still widely used, but there are also lots of ways to deter slugs without poisoning them, and putting the creatures which eat them at risk. For more information about coping with slugs and snails, see page 138.

Weedkillers

Glyphosate is one of the most widely used chemicals in horticulture and is the active ingredient of most of the weedkillers you'll find on the shelves at the garden centre. It is marketed as being quick to degrade in the soil and harmless if used in line with the manufacturers' instructions. However, there is a growing body of evidence that casts doubt on its longer-term impacts on the environment, including damage to bees and persistence in water and the food chain. In studies published in 2013 and 2022, traces of glyphosate were found in the urine of over 70 per cent of people tested in the UK, Germany and America; this is particularly concerning as the compound is regarded as 'probably carcinogenic to humans' by the International Agency for Research on Cancer. While it's currently very hard to completely avoid this ubiquitous substance in our food and farmland, the least we can do is keep it out of our private gardens.

There are a number of other chemicals used in domestic weedkillers for sale in the UK, including ones which kill broadleaved plants in lawns. These also pose risks to human health and the environment, especially if used incorrectly. There are also new products being marketed as 'natural', which are made from seemingly benign ingredients such as acetic acid, a constituent of vinegar. It's hard to know what the long-term effects of these products are likely to be on soil organisms and aquatic life but it's unlikely to be zero. In the end, as with most things, there is no substitute for the hard work of hand-weeding and the common-sense approach to living with some unplanned vegetation. If the job's too big, you may need to get someone in to help you; large spreading plants such as bamboo may even require a mini-digger. If you simply can't keep an area as you want it without regular use

of chemicals, perhaps it's time to rethink the design and planting of that area. This may take the investment of time, energy and possibly money, but it's likely to be better for your health and well-being in the long run, as well as for the environment.

Fertilisers

A lot of traditional gardening manuals recommend the regular application of fertilisers to keep plants in optimal growth. Many of these man-made fertilisers are the result of mining for certain minerals, energy-intensive manufacture or the by-product of industrial farming. They

are also largely unnecessary if soil health has been maintained through good management. Sometimes too much fertiliser will lead to plants becoming overly lush and leafy, making them less resilient to wind and predation from insects. Or, if nutrients are not needed by plants, the surplus might leach through the soil and contaminate groundwater. Where additional nutrition is needed in a vegetable plot or a new border that seems impoverished, mulching with

▲ Gardeners find there is no substitute for hand-weeding. These volunteers at Rainham Hall in London are sharing what can sometimes be an arduous task.

bulky organic matter such as homemade garden compost is the best approach, as this improves the structure of the soil and its water-holding capacity, as well as feeding plant roots and soil micro-organisms. For spot feeding of very hungry crops such as tomatoes or plants growing in containers, it's a great idea to make your own liquid plant food by soaking nettles or comfrey in water for a couple of weeks. These plants are deep-rooted and have the ability to take up a lot of nutrients from the soil, some of which are then released into the water as they rot down.

◀ Comfrey growing in the garden at Acorn Bank in Cumbria.

CHAPTER 4

CARING FOR YOUR GARDEN

CARING FOR YOUR GARDEN

Have you ever wondered if the most sustainable and nature-friendly garden would be one that is left alone completely? Wasteland and abandoned gardens seem to be wonderful habitat for foxes, badgers, hedgehogs, nesting birds and a wealth of invertebrates. Should we step back from our gardens and let nature reclaim them? The answer is that we can if we want to, but they will change quickly and there is much that we need from our gardens – places to rest, play, hang laundry, grow food – which they could not provide if left to grow into scrub.

The ideal solution is to achieve a balance between the aesthetic beauty we enjoy, the amount of order we need, and the benefits our garden can offer to wildlife. This may require weighing up certain factors before we prune or tidy an area, rather than simply following the traditional gardening calendar. In larger gardens it may mean not trying to tame more than we can manage or not gardening right up to the edges. As we tend our gardens through the year, it pays to think of ourselves as simply guiding natural change rather than resisting it altogether. There will be times when we do decide to step in and restore more order, and times when we step back and watch nature at work. This is a far more mindful and stress-free way to garden than battling to maintain a perfect picture in the face of seasonal change and constant growth. It is an approach that also takes the pressure off – your garden is not meant to be under complete control; far better that it is alive and inviting.

DISTURBANCE

Judging exactly how and when to get stuck into gardening tasks is probably the trickiest aspect of gardening for wildlife. Many gardeners are keen naturalists, but few of us can be expected to know the life cycles of all the creatures that share our gardens, and therefore what kinds of disturbance they can tolerate. Some insects have several generations in one year; others only one. Some overwinter as adults; others as pupae, larvae or eggs. Some birds breed in our gardens before moving south for winter, while others come to our gardens in winter having bred further north. The more knowledge of these patterns we can gain the better, but it also pays to simply be sensitive year-round, remembering that just because we can't see creatures doesn't mean they're not there.

The simplest advice is not to make any changes unnecessarily and never all at once. If your garden feels too unruly at a certain time of year, perhaps start by sweeping a path or edging a border – that might be enough to satisfy your desire for order and make the garden look loved again. When you do need to prune or tidy, give some thought to what creatures might be making use of the area, whether they might be vulnerable at that time of year and whether the job can wait for a different season. Timing is everything. Disturbance between March and July could cause a bird to abandon their nest or reveal it to cats, while changes from October to March are likely to disturb overwintering animals. A wide range of mammals, amphibians and invertebrates need a safe, sheltered, frost-free place to survive winter. Some fully hibernate but

◀ Foxes often visit gardens and some may find a spot to breed there if it's sufficiently undisturbed.

▶ Peacock butterflies overwinter as adults and will often hibernate in dry places like garden sheds until March or April ready to breed in summer.

What do I do if I disturb something?

Most creatures are best left close to where you found them to fend for themselves, rather than handled unnecessarily. However, if it's winter and the creature is sleepy, it might not have the energy to move to safety so try to ensure it is covered from the worst weather and hidden from predators. In spring, newly fledged birds are sometimes found on the ground chirping manically. Usually, the mother is nearby and will respond to the cries and keep feeding the chick until it is strong enough to fly. If there are cats in the neighbourhood, keep them out of the garden at this time. If you find an injured bird or mammal there will be wildlife rescue organisations locally that you can seek advice from or take the animal to, but this is very stressful for most animals and should only be done if they are unable to fend for themselves.

many wake up and feed or bask occasionally. So in winter, even a pile of leaves in a corner might have been harbouring life since autumn and is best left alone until spring when creatures using it will be more easily able to cope. In autumn a pile intended for burning should be checked over and restacked before striking a match or, better still, left alone.

Major building and landscaping projects may be necessary at times but will almost certainly set back the populations of creatures using your garden, especially if the works are prolonged. If big changes must be made, try to leave some parts of the garden undisturbed and plan in new features that could offer alternative habitat (as described in Chapter 1). As well as ensuring building projects do not harm protected species, homeowners in England are now legally obliged to prove that any project which requires planning permission will have a net gain for biodiversity. When it comes to tree works, seek expert advice from a qualified arborist who knows about tree species and tree health, not just how to wield a chainsaw safely. They should be able to advise on the likelihood of bat roosts in mature trees as these are legally protected all year round. It's also worth considering other solutions to making trees safe or letting light into a garden besides felling them entirely. In her book, ecologist Jennifer Owen notes that as a result of having had a birch tree in her garden severely pollarded, it died and after that she never once recorded lacewing in her garden again, as they had been dependent on that particular tree.

CUTTING GRASS

As discussed in Chapter 1, some of the plants that grow within lawns can be a great source of nectar and pollen for insects if they are allowed to flower. This can be achieved by mowing only

once every two or three weeks and allowing grass to get a little longer between cuts. Reducing how much you mow also allows grass to withstand drought and wear better, as well as saving energy.

If you are able to leave some areas of grass long throughout the summer to create a meadow area, this is even better for nature as it allows creatures to breed there. The timing and method of cutting then needs to be planned

to take these creatures into consideration. Traditional meadows would grow all spring and early summer, and then be cut for hay in late summer and grazed for a few months. Gardeners are often advised to mimic this by cutting down their meadows between mid-July and September. This tidies them up at a time they may be beginning to get too tall and floppy and allows light into the sward to encourage the wild flowers. However, waiting until late September or even October has many advantages. It will allow more plant species to set seed – including late ones like wild carrot – and leave more time for the species using your meadow to complete

▲ The team at Hidcote in Gloucestershire stopped mowing the grass in the orchard 15 years ago and began to establish this meadow, introducing yellow rattle and other wild flowers.

their life cycles. Butterflies such as meadow browns and gatekeepers lay their eggs in garden meadows in summer so that when they hatch the caterpillars can feed on the grasses. These caterpillars then feed right through into autumn before burrowing down in tussocks of grass to hibernate for the winter. If grasshoppers are present, easily recognisable by their sound, they'll be laying eggs into the soil in your meadow from late summer until autumn, so the later you leave it the better for them too.

When it comes to cutting, try to walk the area first, gently sweeping the grass with a stick to encourage any sheltering creatures such as frogs, slow-worms, voles or moths to move. Ideally, you'll have a border nearby they can escape into. It's also best to cut slowly in sections; a scythe will do less damage than a strimmer, and use less power. Make your first cut quite high (above 10 centimetres) to allow creatures to huddle beneath. Leave cut grass a day or so to give creatures a chance to move out. Don't leave it too long though as the cuttings can smother the grass and add nutrients you don't want. Clear the grass cuttings up gently and add them to your compost heap or make a pile somewhere so that creatures can escape or overwinter there.

After the initial cut, it does pay to mow the grass a few times in autumn, winter or early spring to reduce its vigour and allow light into the sward. If needed, close mowing at these times will weaken grass and encourage wild flowers. However, keeping the blades set higher so that there is always about 5 centimetres of grass is far better for any insects overwintering in the tussocks. Leaving some areas completely uncut is best for these and for other species such as carder bumblebees, which often nest in long grass. You could vary the areas you leave each year so they don't become mats of grass with no room for other plants.

WEEDING

Weeds are just plants growing where we don't want them. In gardens, they can be native or non-native species, but what they tend to have in common is their ability to produce lots of seed which germinates readily. The seed might come from plants within our gardens or from neighbouring gardens and surrounding areas. All seed needs light to germinate, so weeds are only able to grow in the bare soil in our borders, between paving slabs or within gravel. Weeding out these unwanted plants has traditionally been considered a hugely important task in the garden as they have been said to compete with our garden plants for light, water and nutrients. Many people also seem to think that weeds make a garden look messy or unloved and that a nice garden should have no unintended vegetation.

Fortunately, attitudes are changing and many gardeners realise that not all weeds are actually hugely competitive; some are attractive, have value for wildlife and for soil health. Sometimes, the unplanned vegetation that is occupying a dry space under a tree, or a bed you just don't have time to maintain, might as well be

welcomed, as it is certainly better than nothing. Within your borders, as long as the intended plants are growing strongly, they will easily cope with a few interlopers springing up. Some of these unintended plants can even turn out to be useful – a tall, elegant fennel or toadflax, squeezed in between two lower perennials, might add some interest, while shallow-rooted, low-growing celandine and wild strawberries may

▲ Ferns are allowed to grow amongst the flowering plants in the terraces at Acorn Bank, Cumbria.

◄ Ivy-leafed toadflax often colonises damp and shady parts of gardens, growing through cracks in the brickwork where it does no harm.

be smothering the ground beneath taller plants, helping to protect the soil.

The Art of Weeding

Opening our minds to embracing some unintended plants doesn't usually mean weeding can be avoided altogether. All borders require a bit of picking through, especially if you garden in a relaxed way and are tolerant of self-seeding wild flowers like willowherb and herb Robert, or self-seeding garden plants such as forget-me-nots. Fortunately, there are tricks for managing this as efficiently as possible so that it doesn't

become a burden. If you find weeding very uncomfortable, you'll probably need to work in short bursts, moving carefully and using a kneeler, or employ someone to help at key times.

First, it really pays to remove weeds while they are still small and can be pulled out by hand or gently uprooted with a hand fork. Many weeds are quick-growing, short-lived species which don't put down deep roots, but even tougher perennial weeds are fairly easy to remove if caught before they grow substantial roots. There are two main times in the garden calendar when you get a big flush of weeds. The first is when the ground warms up at the start of spring and seeds germinate in bare ground beneath deciduous shrubs or between herbaceous plants before they fill out. The second is around

September when the soil becomes moist and seed that has ripened over the summer germinates wherever there is enough light. Fortunately, these are nice times to be out in the garden, gently working away. Weeding when the soil is moist is best done by hand, or you can use a hand fork if you feel any resistance. This means weeds are less likely to snap off, leaving roots in the ground to regrow, and you're less likely to do damage to the soil structure or

▲ Fast-growing but short-lived plants with uninteresting flowers, like bittercress, are well worth removing as soon as you spot them before they set seed and send up even more seedlings.

▶ Bindweed is a deep-rooted perennial which tangles around other plants. It has lovely flowers so you may want to tolerate it in really wild areas but elsewhere it will need regular pulling and digging out.

neighbouring plants. If you need to weed in dry conditions, you can hoe off very young weed seedlings and leave them to shrivel where they are. As long as you don't disturb the soil surface again, you shouldn't get too many more. Regular hoeing in dry weather is the best way to keep on top of weeds in veg beds, which often have bare soil prone to unwanted interlopers.

There will be times when you need to remove more deeply rooted perennials because they have escaped notice or spread by root from under a neighbour's fence. These are best dug out with a border fork with as much root as you can get. If it's not possible to get a fork into the border because the soil is baked dry or it would disturb a neighbouring plant, you can just break

perennial weeds off at soil level by hand, using a weeding knife, hoe or even a strimmer. This will weaken them temporarily but they will grow back from roots left in the ground, so make a note to revisit the area and do a thorough job at a better time. In the lawn it really pays to use a fork to remove tap-rooted weeds like dandelions, docks or plantain if they are proliferating. In damp soil in spring or autumn, this can be satisfying job. Just put a border fork beneath, lever it until you feel the root release from the ground, let go and then pull the whole plant with its root out by hand and tread the hummock you've created back down. Bare patches will soon fill in with grasses.

Especially tricky spots to weed include gravel areas and paving. If you have soil in your gravel or no membrane beneath it, weeds are inevitable and it's probably best to accept some. Do they really matter in a car parking area? If you do need to remove them, you can try pulling by hand but may end up needing to use a hand fork or border fork. Once an area is clear you can try raking the gravel from time to time to stop other seedlings getting established. For weeding between paving slabs, a weeding knife is really useful. Unless you are planning to fill the gaps with mortar it's a good idea to introduce some low-growing plants that you want between your paving slabs so that you aren't just endlessly clearing them. Wall bellflower (*Campanula portenschlagiana*) is good for a semi-shaded spot while Mexican fleabane (*Erigeron karvinskianus*) and creeping thyme (*Thymus serpyllum*) do well in sun.

▼ Mexican fleabane growing in the steps at Canons Ashby, Northamptonshire.

▶ Weeding in a comfortable position for an hour or so each day can be a surprisingly pleasant activity.

Mindful Weeding

Many gardeners really enjoy weeding, as it involves getting down among the plants where you can appreciate their beauty and structure, and see how they are growing. The most straightforward approach is to simply clear all unwanted vegetation out from around garden plants. However, this will remove everything, including some seedlings of welcome self-seeders like forget-me-nots, evening primrose, foxgloves, love-in-a-mist, honesty and Mexican fleabane, so it pays to get the hang of identifying these when they are still seedlings, enabling you to leave a few scattered through a border, or even lift and pot spares up to give away. Learning which are your most common weed seedlings also allows you to identify the source; if it's growing in your garden, consider dead-heading in summer as the flowers fade and before they set seed to reduce the number of unwanted seedlings you get in future. This is a very good idea if you are leaving highly vigorous natives like ragwort, willowherb and dock. Always check for larvae if pulling out a stand of a native plant like willowherb, as it can support several moth and butterfly species.

Weeding with your eyes open like this also provides an opportunity to study the plant community in your garden – what's doing well and what might be out of balance. While healthy plants that look after themselves is what you want, plants that spread too quickly are something to be wary of. Some garden plants are covered by legislation because their invasive nature means they are causing serious problems in the countryside; others have the potential to become so now or in the future with climate change. If a non-native plant in your garden is springing up as seedlings in all your borders or spreading quickly from the clump you initially planted, it would be wise to keep an eye on it and even go so far as to remove it if your garden is close to an area of countryside. You may be able to manage it now, but what will happen in the future when your garden is cared for by someone else or not cared for at all? Plants that thrive on neglect may leave a legacy on the landscape that we gardeners didn't intend.

CUTTING BACK BORDERS

One of the most familiar activities in the gardener's calendar is the cutting down and tidying up of our borders in autumn – often referred to benignly as 'putting them to bed for winter'. This can be a hugely satisfying task, which removes all signs of autumn decay from the garden, leaving a blank canvas ready for the following spring. However, this is something divorced from the natural process. In nature, vegetation dies back, feeding detritivores and returning nutrients to plant roots and to the soil, with fallen leaves protecting the soil surface and new growth. A mass of still-standing dead vegetation also provides seedheads for birds and hollow stems or other dry hiding places for invertebrates, amphibians and small mammals trying to get through the winter.

You may feel that by removing stems to the compost heap, the creatures can go with them, but in fact many will be squashed or exposed to weather and predators by the process of cutting back, or find themselves trapped in rotting vegetation on the heap rather than the dry place they had intended. It is far better to leave plants standing as habitat until well into the new year. Many will actually reward you by being highly architectural and providing winter interest. Cutting back is also easier after winter as many stems will simply pull away with no need for secateurs.

When you do need to tidy up, do it in stages and try always to have an area of permanent cover that creatures can escape into or you can relocate them to. Start with areas closest to the house or paths that you use in winter – tidying here may give you the sense of order you need, allowing all else to remain wild. By late February you may want to clear other areas you can see from paths or windows in order to expose early flowering bulbs. Do this with extreme caution as creatures disturbed now may struggle to relocate. You could just cut stems back to about 20 centimetres, so there is some vegetation present for stem- and tussock-dwelling creatures, or you could chop and drop what you cut onto the surface of the soil as an instant mulch or make piles of cuttings in the back of borders to provide habitat right through into summer. In March it's tempting to clear everything else to let new growth come through, but go gently, especially if it's a late, cold spring. Creatures like the fat green caterpillar of the angle shades moth, which are often disturbed from their winter hiding spots at this time of year, may still be a few weeks away from making the transformation into an adult capable of producing the next generation.

▶ In winter and early spring, weed and tidy with caution as lots of creatures will still be trying to hide somewhere sheltered to survive the cold weather.

Perennials that look great left standing through winter

◄ Achillea 'Coronation Gold'
Long after these flat yellow flower heads have faded, they stand up tall, often topped with frost or snow.

◄ Phlomis russeliana
Needs a lot of space when in flower and leaf but pays you back with these characterful seedheads which last for months.

◄ Veronicastrum virginicum
These tall, thin candelabra-shaped flower heads are just as good dead and dry as they are in flower.

◄ Aruncus dioicus
Finishes flowering in early summer but if you can leave the heads; they'll look great again in autumn and winter.

◄ Hylotelephium × mottramianum 'Herbstfreude'
A classic garden plant with seedheads which will survive all weathers to be standing strong in spring the following year.

◄ Rudbeckia fulgida var. deamii
A brilliant yellow flower for autumn with upright stems and neat, dark seedheads which last into winter.

▶ Try to mulch with compost generated within your own garden. Not everywhere needs mulching each year, so you can do areas in rotation.

MULCHING AND SOIL HEALTH

After the traditional autumn cut back, gardening manuals often tell us to mulch the bare soil with compost or manure annually to enrich it and protect it from the elements. However, research is finding that our shrub and flower borders do not need a thick layer of compost each year and soil health can be pretty well maintained by having permanent plant roots in the ground and some fallen leaf litter. Over-feeding beds can lead to soft, sappy plants that require support and to leaching of surplus nutrients into ground water. While mulching does help soils store carbon, most soils can only store so much, and the surplus is lost into the atmosphere. It's also worth being aware that if the organic matter that you use needs to be transported to you using fossil fuels, more carbon will be burnt in that process than your soil will ever sequester.

So, when you do mulch, aim to use your own compost generated within your garden and use it where it's most needed. Some of the best places are the vegetable garden where soil gets depleted by harvesting; around newly planted shrubs, trees and perennials; and anywhere with compacted or heavy soils. If you have enough compost, mulch established shrub and flower borders on rotation every three years or more. This can be done in March, following a spring cut back.

Equally important for soil health is avoiding compaction by not walking or driving on bare soil excessively, especially when it is wet. Compaction removes air pores, reduces water-holding capacity and damages soil biology. If there is an area of soil you need to walk on a lot to access a part of your border, consider adding stepping stones or a layer of woodchip. Soil structure and biology is also damaged by working the soil, especially when it is very wet or dry. This is another reason why permanent planting schemes are preferable to seasonal bedding and

Earthworms

The biggest and most familiar creature in the soil is the earthworm and we have long known that healthy soils have good populations of earthworms. There are 31 species of earthworm in Britain and Ireland, 16 of which may be found in gardens. They can be grouped into three types: those that tunnel up and down like the familiar common earthworm (*Lumbricus terrestris*); the ones that create more branching horizontal burrows within the top 30–50 centimetres of soil and are pale-coloured; and those that live in the soil surface among leaf litter and are darker coloured. All are crucially important for aerating the soil and moving organic matter down from the surface into the soil. You do not need to introduce earthworms to your soil – they will come if it is not overly compacted or disturbed and there is organic matter from mulches or leaf litter.

why many people practice 'no dig' vegetable gardening (see Chapter 5, page 170).

We are only just beginning to understand the complexity of soil biology and how different fungi and bacteria support the growth and resilience of plant roots. Plants do not only use the nutrients in the soil taken up by their roots, they create their own nutrients by converting sunlight into energy and then excrete some sugars out into the soil via their roots. These sugars feed soil micro-organisms that help process plant matter in the soil into nutrients and even break down rocks into minerals, which are then available for the roots to take up. Some fungal organisms known as mycorrhizae actually grow into and around plant roots, increasing their surface area to assist with water and nutrient uptake, and help to make them resistant to soil-borne diseases. There are now mycorrhizal products available to buy for adding to your soil on planting, which some gardeners swear by, but it's not fully proven that these complex symbiotic relationships can be recreated on demand with a generic product.

▶ Compaction around the roots of trees causes stress to trees but mulching makes a big difference, protecting the ground and boosting soil biology as it breaks down.

PRUNING

Traditional gardening teaches us how to restrain many garden shrubs and climbers from becoming their natural size and shape with regular pruning. Sensitively done, this can ensure plants remain bushy with flowers and berries carried at eye-level rather than high up. Insensitively done, it can lead to very unnaturally shaped plants with reduced flowering and fruiting. Pruning of garden trees can be particularly cruel, leading to ugly vertical regrowth and sometimes wounds that don't heal well and allow disease to enter.

In a nature-friendly garden, shrubs and climbers needn't all be confined to small spaces. Large plants with thick, gnarly stems and canopies that blend together have more to offer in terms of nesting and hiding spaces for wildlife;

while fruit and flowers high up may be exactly where pollinating insects and birds want them. Some plants might not need to be pruned at all while others might only need it if they are beginning to block a view or a pathway. Taller shrubs and trees actually provide an opportunity for more layers of vegetation beneath them, meaning the overall plant mass in the garden is greater. Cutting down on pruning also means less work and fewer prunings to deal with afterwards.

When you do need to prune be aware that timing is crucial. First, it is important to avoid the bird-nesting season, which starts in March and can run until August, with the most important months being April, May and June. If you need to prune within that period,

▲ When you do need to prune, do it cautiously, especially if plants are about to flower or have berries on that could be food for birds over winter.

stressful time for them to go without leaves and be able to quickly grow more.

With all this in mind, it really pays to find out the names of all your shrubs and trees and look up their individual pruning requirements in a trustworthy guide before grabbing the loppers. Some trees never respond well – birch and cherries frequently succumb to disease and die after hard or repeated pruning.

When it comes to pruning technique, a common mistake is cutting across the top of the plant at the height you want it to be. This is fine for a hedge but rarely works for individual trees and shrubs as most will simply respond with vigorous vertical growth from the cut ends. More sensitive approaches are removing lower branches to let in light and views beneath the canopy; removing older stems from the base to let younger ones take over, or lightly trimming back to a well-placed side shoot. There are also a few plants that can be cut hard back to the base, usually at the start of the year. These include many roses, late-flowering clematis and buddleia, as well as willow and dogwood grown for stem colour, or elder and smoke bush grown purely for their foliage.

PLANTING

Even in a gently managed garden there are usually exciting opportunities to introduce new plants or replant divisions from the ones you have. When you get this chance and have chosen your new plant carefully (there's lots of advice in Chapter 2), do be aware that there's a lot more to planting than making a hole in the ground and pushing the roots into it. So many plants fail in their first year, either because the ground was not prepared properly, the plant was planted too deep or too shallow, or they dried out in the months after planting. Success with planting

you'll need to check plants carefully for nests before commencing work and delay if you find one. Second, some plants are very sensitive to pruning at certain times as they may bleed sap afterwards – grape vines, for example, are best pruned in early winter, while magnolias are best pruned in summer. Finally, sensitive timing also ensures maximum flowers for pollinating insects and for us. In general, deciduous shrubs that flower in winter, spring or early summer will need to be pruned immediately after flowering, leaving them the rest of summer to put on new growth, which will ripen and flower the next year. Deciduous shrubs that flower in mid- to late summer or autumn can be pruned in winter or early spring, as they'll have time to put on new growth afterwards, which will ripen and flower later the same year. Most evergreens should be pruned in early to mid-spring as it's the least

▲ It's easy to accidentally disturb nesting birds when pruning in spring or summer so try to prune before March or after July and check carefully for nests first.

means thinking about the roots and what they need to grow in their new location.

It's best to start off with plants that have strong, healthy roots and a good ratio of roots to leaves. Big plants raised in small pots are likely to struggle when first planted, as the small, congested root system will need to support a lot of leaves. These might benefit from a trim of their top growth and gentle teasing out of congested roots before planting. Young plants that have experienced no stress usually establish best and bareroot shrubs often do well (as outlined on page 84). If you choose to treat yourself to something bigger like a semi-mature tree or shrub, it will need extra care during and after planting.

Soil moisture is crucial, both when you plant and for the months afterwards while the roots are establishing their connections with the soil structure and biology. Try to plant when the soil is wet but not saturated – 24 hours after heavy rain is ideal. Spring planting when the soil is warm and moist is good, and this is usually the time when the garden centres are full of tempting plants. However, autumn planting is even better for most hardy plants, as the soil around the roots is likely to remain moist for many months with no risk of a drought around the corner. If you do have to plant into a dry soil for some reason, place the plant in its hole and then fill the hole with water and let it drain down before backfilling the soil around the rootball and watering again. This is known as 'puddling in'. If you have to plant in very wet conditions, put planks or stepping stones down to stand on so you don't compact the soil with your feet.

When you create your planting hole, it needs to be wider than the rootball you are planting, and free from other plant roots. If the roots of neighbouring plants are filling the space, it's probably not suitable for planting into as new plants can rarely compete with ones that are already established. Traditional gardening wisdom had us adding fertiliser and lots of compost to the planting hole, but this is increasingly being regarded as unnecessary and even harmful at times. You can add some homemade garden compost to the bottom of your planting hole to feed the soil biology. Don't add a huge amount as this may hold too much water or rot down and cause the plant to sink and be planted deeper than you intended, which can be damaging to some plants, especially trees. Mulching around the base of the plant after planting is usually better to keep the area weed-free and trap in moisture. However, if your soil is healthy, most plants will be fine without, and some drought-tolerant Mediterranean species would actually prefer not to have rich, soggy compost around them.

▶ Think about the roots of your plants and what they need to grow in their new location.

Don't remove – renovate!

Sometimes a shrub, tree or climber may outgrow its allotted space and be causing some problems among electricity cables or getting under the eaves of buildings. In these cases, it may be possible to renovate the plant rather than removing it. Renovation usually involves cutting the plant down hard in winter or early spring and hoping it will send up new shoots from the stump over the course of the spring and summer. Once these new shoots get going the mature root system will mean the plant is soon back to a reasonable size. This is so much more sustainable than digging out the roots and buying a new plant. Many deciduous species including buddleia, roses, hazel, dogwood, willow, honeysuckle, *Clematis montana* and even wisteria will tolerate this. Some tough evergreens such as camellias and cotoneasters will too, but a handful, such as *Ceanothus* and *Cistus* won't, so it pays to research this first.

▶ *Clematis montana*

▲ Raking leaves from the lawn in autumn can help to keep grass healthy but it isn't necessary to remove leaves from all beds and borders.

CLEANING AND TIDYING

It is unrealistic to expect an outdoor space to be as clean and tidy as a house. Algae, moss, mould, fungi and mildew are all part of the natural world and using cleaning products to remove them will inevitably have an impact on other organisms. If these things are causing a genuine problem, such as making a path dangerously slippery, they can usually be removed with a stiff brush or pressure washer. Many people spend a lot of time collecting leaves when in fact they do no harm building up under hedges or even on borders. When they do need to be cleared from paths and lawns, do it promptly rather than leaving them to become home to creatures and then destroying it. Try to use a broom or rake rather than a leaf blower or sucker, which are noisy and destructive. If there are areas within the garden you need to tidy up – piles of pots or debris, for example – do this in summer or early autumn, before the cold weather sets in; this is probably better than allowing it to offer refuge and then disrupting it in winter.

High standards of hygiene to avoid introducing pathogens into a garden are important in professional horticulture and gardens with rare plant collections, but at home all that matters is a bit of common sense. Avoiding wearing your gardening boots to other gardens or areas of countryside, or cleaning them between visits, is very responsible as there are a number of soil-borne diseases around that can be spread by muddy footwear. Keeping tools clean and dry is good for them and stops you unknowingly spreading diseases around the garden; disinfecting them is probably only necessary after pruning something you know to be diseased, like a fruit tree with canker. Washing greenhouses down with water at the end of the growing season or at the start of the next keeps the glass clean but scrubbing every nook and cranny, disturbing

every living thing hiding there, is probably
only necessary if you've had an outbreak of a
greenhouse pest like red spider mite. Keeping
pots and propagation areas orderly and dry
makes sense, but there's no need to clean them
all unless you've experienced a problem such as
damping off of seedlings. Positioning water butts
in the shade with lids on keeps the water cool
and reduces the likelihood of them harbouring
pathogens, but you could also scrub them down
every few years when they are empty, especially if
the water has become stagnant at any point.

Cleaning Ponds

Ponds should be left alone as much as possible, as
they will have creatures using them all year round,
but it is sometimes necessary to lift and divide
overcrowded vegetation, remove algae or repair a
punctured liner. Pond plants are best dealt with
in mid-spring but check for frog or toad spawn
first. Blanket weed may need to be skimmed off
with a rake or net little and often throughout the
spring and summer months, and fallen leaves or
dead plant material might need to be removed
in autumn. Any vegetation pulled out of a pond
should be taken a little at a time. If you put it
into a bucket of pond or rainwater, you can check
it for life there before scooping it back out and
putting it next to the pond in the hope that any
creatures you have missed can crawl out and get
back into the water. Major works to a pond are
probably best done in November, especially if you
have newts. If you have to disrupt the bottom,
keep the sediment in buckets to put back in as it
may be full of overwintering life.

▶ For many years this shallow, concrete-lined
ornamental pond at Dyffryn Gardens in the Vale of
Glamorgan was being drained and cleaned annually to
keep it free of blanket weed, but the garden team have
now stopped doing this so that dragonflies can complete
their life cycle. They have also added more plants to
help absorb nutrients and keep the water clean, and
now the blanket weed is naturally under control.

MANAGING PLANT HEALTH PROBLEMS

If you look after your soil, choose plants well suited to your garden and practise sensible hygiene, your plants should remain largely healthy. It also pays to rethink what constitutes a problem and not expect plants to be spotless.

Plant Diseases

Many plant diseases are widespread in the environment and cannot be completely avoided or controlled. A few spotted leaves or a section of dieback on a well-established plant is usually nothing to worry about; the plant will often look great again when wetter weather comes or new growth is produced.

You can try to break some cycles of disease such as rose black spot by clearing up fallen leaves from beneath the plant where the spores would otherwise overwinter ready to reinfect. These are best burnt, buried, binned or taken to the tip and not composted. You may also find that mulching to keep plant roots more moist can help. Fortunately, many common plant diseases such as rusts and leaf spots are restricted to certain species so you needn't worry that the disease will spread around your garden. If a particular plant looks ill each summer, it may just be easiest to give up and try something else. There are so many lovely bomb-proof garden plants!

The times to be most concerned are if an established woody plant dies suddenly, as this may mean it has a root disease such as phytophthora or honey fungus, which could spread to other woody plants. Fortunately, old-fashioned treatments for these kinds of diseases, which harmed soil biology and leached into watercourses, are no longer available and now

▼ The sudden decline of rhododendrons may be a sign of a serious problem such as the fungal disease *Phytophthora ramorum*.

our best bet is to remove as many of the diseased roots as we can and plant something different.

Another cause for concern is if a newly purchased plant begins to look very ill, despite your good care. If there's a chance this plant could have been imported, it may have brought a new disease with it. That's why buying British is a good idea for peace of mind (see page 86).

Rethinking Pests

We used to refer to the creatures that visited our gardens and did any kind of damage as 'pests' but many gardeners are beginning to recognise this is an unhealthy view. Many of these 'pests' are in fact native creatures trying to find the resources they need for survival. Most are only an issue for a short window in their life cycle and few cause lasting damage to plants. Their populations often vary greatly from year to year depending on weather conditions and the availability of food or predators. This is why one year your honeysuckle might be beset with blackfly and another year there's no sign of it at all. Try to relax about it and think of it this way: if your plants are playing a full role in the ecosystem of your garden, they probably *should* be getting nibbled!

Of course, there are times when damage from bigger visitors such as pigeons, squirrels, rabbits, badgers or deer is very frustrating. Some of these creatures can seriously knock a plant back in one visit. With this in mind, whenever you introduce a new plant to your garden consider what might take an interest in it. Prevention is always better than cure and can save a lot of heartbreak so it's worth erecting barriers around vulnerable plants. If you can't fence rabbits and deer out entirely, you may need to restrict your plant palette to species they are not interested in.

Aphids

There are over 500 species of aphid in Britain, and they are a really valuable food source for many creatures, including hoverflies, lacewing, ladybirds and blue tits. Their sap sucking usually only does temporary harm to a plant and they are often quite specific about their hosts and therefore unlikely to spread from plant to plant. Many only smother a specific plant for a few days in spring before birds and other predators start picking them off. As outlined in Chapter 3, resorting to sprays often kills non-target insects and removes a food source for predators, which then won't be around to control the aphids next time. A better approach is to watch and wait – if no predators appear and the plant really is declining, try squashing the aphids manually or blasting them with the hose if you must.

Coping with slugs and snails

Slugs and snails are one of the biggest challenges gardeners face. Unfortunately, if you garden for nature, with plenty of plant cover and undisturbed nooks and crannies, it is likely you will have lots of them. There are approximately 44 terrestrial slugs and 99 land snails found in the UK, but thankfully not all of them feed on living plants and many serve the important function of breaking down debris. They also serve a role as food for birds, amphibians and small mammals, though admittedly perhaps not in the quantities we would like!

In warm, damp spring weather when new shoots are emerging from many plants, slugs and snails can drive gardeners to distraction, making the garden feel like a bit of a battlefield. Trying to win this war and eliminate them is not sustainable and can take a lot of the joy out of gardening. Instead, it's best to know their habits and be a step ahead. New shoots on a range of plants are palatable so it pays to keep watch and be ready to protect these with some

Options for protecting vulnerable plants from slugs and snails include:

Wool pellets, vermiculite or sharp sand as a barrier around plants	This works well if you put enough but will need topping up every few days. Some recommend coffee but use in moderation to avoid negatively affecting soil bacteria and other organisms.
Beer traps placed near vulnerable plants	These are highly effective but rather cruel and they may occasionally catch beetles and other insects too.
Nematodes	Great for reducing soil-dwelling slugs from a contained bed; not intended for use across the whole garden.
Copper tape and/or grease around the rims of pots	There are mixed views on the effectiveness of copper tape but many report success with grease. Just make sure the barrier isn't compromised by leaves.
Raised beds	Tall-sided beds can deter molluscs from finding plants so are really useful for growing veg. Keep any grass around the beds short to remove hiding places.
Grow plants in metal pots, e.g. galvanised	Good for plants like hostas and salads, which will grow in pots.
Check plants on damp evenings and pick off slugs and snails	Can help if done regularly, but captured molluscs will need to be killed or moved some distance away.
Organic slug pellets	Best restricted to use in cold frames and under netted crops so that birds don't take them.

Plants most loved by slugs and snails

There are a number of plants that seem to be so palatable to slugs and snails that they will actively seek them out, overcoming barriers or traps and often decimating new shoots as quickly as they emerge. Even once well-established, some of these plants don't seem to build up the toughness or bitterness to deter molluscs. These favourites include clematis, hosta (shown above), delphiniums, *Salvia* 'Caradonna', *Rudbeckia* 'Herbstsonne' and *Eupatorium purpureum*. Plants with fleshy flower stalks that are frequently chewed through just as buds emerge include most irises, daylilies and some of the daintier red-hot pokers. In sunny gardens with soil that dries out on the surface, you may be able to grow them, but in damp gardens with lots of dense vegetation, it's a losing battle best given up on.

Slug- and snail-proof ornamental plants

The most stress-free way of tackling slugs and snails is to stick to growing plants they just don't seem interested in. Fortunately, there are tonnes of these including *Hylotelephium*, *Oreganum*, *Thalictrum* (pictured), *Sanguisorba*, *Epimedium*, *Euphorbia*, *Geum*, peonies, *Alchemilla*, fennel, *Persicaria*, *Cephalaria*, *Knautia*, *Aruncus*, *Ligularia*, *Phlomis*, *Lysimachia*, *Achillea*, geraniums, lungwort, *Rodgersia*, *Astrantia*, *Veronicastrum*, *Stachys*, *Libertia*, *Penstemon*, *Amsonia*, Japanese anemones and *Erysimum*, as well as most ferns and grasses.

kind of barrier until the growth thickens up and develops resistance. Plants that have been recently planted are often very vulnerable so it's wise to also take protective measures for these until they get established and become less of a target. One of the easiest protective measures is to do as much planting as you can in autumn as the weather cools down and molluscs become less active. This can allow plants to get their roots down over winter and be more resilient by the time spring comes around. If you do have to plant in spring or summer, as with many veg plants and annuals, make sure plants coming out of the greenhouse have been acclimatised to outdoors gradually so they are not too soft and vulnerable.

DEALING WITH WASTE

Ecological gardening practices, such as not being too tidy, buying less bedding and restricting the size of your lawn, may well reduce the amount of waste plant material you generate in your garden each year. There will, however, always be a certain amount and it's important to make use of this within your garden. Putting it in a garden waste bin, or taking it to the tip, means all those resources are leaving your garden and fossil fuels are being used in their transport and processing. Burning woody waste may seem like the easiest solution for those with big gardens, but this doesn't recycle the nutrients and instead releases carbon into the atmosphere.

Having a compost heap is a brilliant way to recycle most plant material from the garden, and you can add in veg peelings from the kitchen and straw or woodchip bedding from chickens or other pets if you have them. Almost any plant debris can be composted if you chop it up finely enough. The finer you chop it the hotter your compost heap will get and the quicker ingredients will break down. Compost heaps that get hot are good for killing the roots and seeds of unwanted plants as well as spores of plant diseases. If you have a very small garden, a 'Dalek' or small bin that you add to from above while taking useful compost from beneath may be sufficient. However, having two or three compost bays is far easier, so you can be filling one while the other is breaking down or being used. Turning the material from one bin into the other will also help it heat up and break down more quickly and thoroughly, although this is heavy work and not strictly necessary.

It's a good idea to get into the hang of separating different types of waste plant material

▶ Composting areas are the powerhouses of the garden and needn't look unattractive.

as you work rather than allowing a huge pile of assorted debris to build up and overwhelm you. Try to have a barrow or trug and a smaller bucket or pot on the go. The larger container is for your easily compostable stuff, which ideally you chop as you fill it; the smaller one is for more problematic waste: the roots of troublesome perennial weeds like bindweed or the seedheads of over-vigorous seeders like dandelions. This less compostable waste could either be taken to the tip once or twice a year, where it will be composted at much hotter temperatures than you can probably achieve at home. Or you can soak it in a bucket of water for a few weeks to make sure it's well rotted down before adding it to your heap.

If you're doing a job that generates woody material, you can remove the thinner side shoots and chop them into the compost, and leave the thicker, straighter material to use as stakes or make into a habitat pile. Alternatively, if you do this a lot, you may wish to invest in a shredder

to allow you to chip it all before adding to the compost heap or for use as a woody mulch under shrubs or on paths. If you end up pruning a plant that is showing signs of disease, such as canker on a fruit tree, it is wise to separate these prunings out and either burn them or take them to the council green waste, which gets hot enough to kill most plant diseases.

When you add these ingredients to your compost heap it's ideal to get a good mix of soft, green material and drier brown material. Greens include kitchen waste, lawn clippings and weeds; browns are dry stems, woody material, straw and pet bedding. When you finish a spell of gardening it's common to have a lot of one type of thing at a time, whether that be dry prunings in autumn, succulent weeds in spring or lawn clippings in summer. You can stack these to one side until you have another material in order to fill your compost with different layers, but this isn't always practical, so don't worry too much – as long as it doesn't get bone dry, or wet and stinky, all heaps will compost down in time.

◀ Autumn leaves can be added to your compost bin but can also be put into their own bin or bagged up and left to rot down separately. They'll make a lovely light compost known as leaf mould, which is ideal for making your own potting compost.

Council garden waste collections

Garden waste that is sent off in a wheelie bin or taken to the tip is usually moved to a specialist site to be composted in huge piles. It is shredded so gets very hot, killing off weeds and pathogens, and is turned frequently to ensure it is a nice, even product. It is then often sold back to gardeners mixed into potting composts or for use as a soil improver. This sounds like a great circular system but unfortunately there are several things that make it less than ideal. Fossil fuels are used in its transport and processing and plastics for bagging it up. Composting sites have to have lots of concrete infrastructure to make them environmentally compliant and prevent them contaminating watercourses. Plus, after all that effort, the end product is less than perfect as it contains microplastics from all the plant labels and packaging people allow to fall in with their green waste, and contaminants from weedkillers that are so commonly used. For anyone with absolutely no space to compost, green bins may be the only option, but for everyone else do stop and think about how much more sense it makes to let this green waste rot down in a corner of the garden from where we can apply it directly back onto the soil.

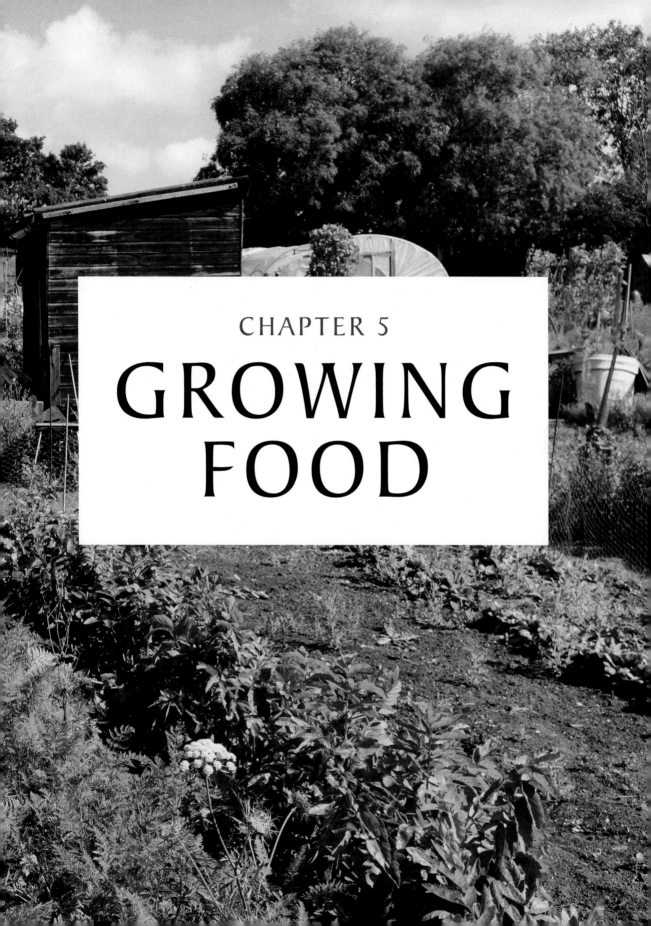

CHAPTER 5

GROWING FOOD

GROWING FOOD

Growing your own food can be enormously rewarding. It's the ultimate hobby – giving you exercise, fresh air and new skills, while also yielding tasty, organically grown, extremely fresh, packaging-free produce. Since much modern farming requires significant input of fertilisers, water and pesticides, creates high carbon emissions and is linked to the pollution of our watercourses, growing some of your own food so that you can buy a little less also has tangible

environmental benefits. Vegetable gardens may not be the most wildlife-friendly part of a garden but the role they play in feeding us can more than compensate for this.

If you don't have the space to create any veg beds in your garden, why not put your name down for an allotment? Or you could look into getting involved in a community food growing project. This can be a lovely, sociable experience and means that for just a few hours' input each week, you learn new skills and get to take produce away.

SELF-SUFFICIENCY

When councils first set up allotments in the 19th century it was to enable poor labourers to feed themselves, as many had lost access to land and were working in industrial jobs with no welfare system to support them. Allotments then were usually 250 square metres (about the same as the total area of a tennis court) which was thought to be sufficient to grow enough vegetables to feed a family. The family would have spent a significant proportion of their free time working the allotment to ensure every inch of the land was as productive as possible, and they would be used to eating simply, with whatever was in season.

Today there are very few people growing and eating like this. It takes a great deal of work, and dedication to harvesting and storing produce during the long winter months when little is coming out of the garden. However, approximately 330,000 people in the UK do have allotments and many more grow food at home. For most of these people, growing fruit and veg is a hobby that they manage to fit into their busy lives. Few are dependent on what they grow but they will almost all be making meaningful harvests between June until October. Talk to anyone doing this and they will usually tell you their produce makes them feel proud and often tastes far better than what they can buy in the supermarket.

◀ Gardens and allotments of all sizes can yield harvests that will save you a few trips to the shop.

The key to ensuring your veg plot makes a meaningful difference to your shopping list is to learn which plants grow well in your garden with the time and facilities you have available; those which will definitely be eaten by you and your family, and what quantities are needed so that your harvests are neither too meagre nor too overwhelming. For ultimate success, be ready to adapt your meals a little to ensure your homegrown produce is placed front and centre, where it deserves to be.

▶ Allotments, like these ones at Coniston Hall in Cumbria, offer the chance to learn new skills, make new friends and take your own produce home.

▼ No packaging or fossil fuels are involved when vegetables can be harvested straight from the garden. A chef at Bateman's in East Sussex picks greens for use in the tearoom.

GETTING STARTED

If you only have access to a balcony or paved courtyard, you can grow a good number of herbs and some vegetables in large containers. This is a great way to get started, as it's easy to remember to water plants right outside your back door, and pots are easier to keep free of slugs and snails than crops in the ground. Outdoor cucumbers can be especially rewarding, as are cut-and-come-again salads and climbing beans if you give them enough water.

However, for most people wishing to reduce what they buy and eat what they grow, access to the soil is crucial. An area of ground 1 metre by 2 metres is enough to produce some salads in early summer, followed by a crop of climbing beans or a couple of courgette plants. Three to four beds of this size will give two people many of the vegetables they need throughout the summer months. More than that and you will be looking at producing enough to feed a family, have fruit bushes and be able to store crops for winter use. Beds will need to be positioned in a sunny position, out of the wind and not on top of tree roots. Although sustainable vegetable growing involves watering as sparingly and strategically as possible (see Chapter 3, page 98) it's inevitable some irrigation will be needed, either for new crops that are putting down roots or established crops growing during drought, so do think about where the nearest water point is. Unfortunately, a small water butt on a shed will soon run dry in a drought, so you may need to ensure you can run a hose from a tap or a larger rainwater storage facility.

Building raised beds is quite an easy way to lay out a vegetable patch. By enclosing the growing areas and having permanent paths in between, you avoid walking on the soil and compacting it. The neatly delineated edges can also help reduce slugs and snails finding their way into your beds. Edges don't need to be especially high – one board's width is enough – but if you make them higher it can give you a more comfortable working position when you're leaning into them and make access even harder for slugs and snails. Keep beds to a maximum of 1.2 metres wide so that they're easy to reach into from either side. Try to use recycled

▲ Vegetable beds with wooden sides can help keep slugs and snails away from your crops and stop you needing to walk on the soil.

boards where possible, but if buying new ones look for wood that is labelled as Grown in Britain, FSC or PEFC, which shows it has been harvested sustainably.

If you are taking over a well-loved allotment or converting a flower bed to veg growing, you should be able to fork out the former crop, cover the ground in a thick layer of garden compost or locally sourced well-rotted manure and start growing. If the patch is thick with grass or other vegetation that is hard to remove, you may want to smother it with some plain brown cardboard, then put a very thick layer of compost on top and grow something tough like potatoes, courgettes or pumpkins in it for a year while the vegetation beneath the cardboard dies back.

Crop rotation

Many guides to vegetable gardening will encourage you to organise your crops into family groups, growing each group together in one bed and rotating the crop each year so that the same crop is not grown in the same place year after year. This is a great principle for farming as different crops tend to cultivate the soil to different depths, utilise different nutrients and attract different insects or diseases. However, in a small plot it's less important, as most crops will end up being close to each other and moved about from time to time. The key thing is to be able to fit in as much as possible and use any gaps which emerge as one crop is harvested. How to do this comes with practice but will also vary from year to year depending on the seasons so don't get too hung up on it.

WHAT TO GROW

If you look in a seed catalogue or a rack of seeds in the garden centre the choice is overwhelming, but it's wise to start with crops you know and love, and can easily use in the kitchen. If you're new to veg growing, perhaps choose just five to start with. Check the back of the packet to see if they can be direct sown outside, which is super easy, or if you will need a greenhouse or sunny windowsill to start them off.

If space is limited, it makes sense to steer clear of staple crops like maincrop potatoes and onions, which you'll never be able to grow enough of to last the year. With other fairly common vegetables like carrots or courgettes, you might want to try interesting varieties with colours, shapes or flavours you can't find in the shops.

You may also wish to look for seed that has been produced organically, is from heritage varieties or has been saved by community seed-saving projects. This is a great way to support sustainable seed production and keep unusual varieties alive.

▼ As you get more confident with growing from seed, you could look into growing and saving heritage varieties, as they do in the walled garden at Knightshayes Court in Devon.

Recommended Veg

These easy crops can be started outside as soon as the soil begins to warm up in March or April.

These veg are also easy to grow but, because they hate the cold, you need to sow them in pots on

◄ Lettuce
Varieties like 'Salad Bowl' or mixed leaves intended for cut-and-come-again are easier and use less space than growing whole lettuces with hearts.

◄ Climbing beans
Runner beans are an age-old favourite, but climbing French beans are much more versatile in the kitchen.

◄ Carrots
Choose the shorter stump-rooted varieties if your soil is very stony, or has lumps of clay, compost or manure.

◄ Courgettes
Yellow varieties are fun. Always grow more than one plant as there need to be enough flowers for bees to cross-pollinate them.

◄ Beetroot
Super-easy to grow with very few pests. Choose traditional, deep red varieties or mixes containing brighter red and white roots.

◄ New potatoes
Choose a first early variety so that they can be harvested in mid-summer, leaving time to sow another crop in the same space.

◄ Rainbow chard
A really beautiful crop that you can harvest for many months of the year. Much easier than spinach.

◄ Spring onions
The perfect addition to your potato salad; a row of these can be harvested little by little over a couple of months.

a windowsill or in a greenhouse and then plant them out in the ground at the start of summer.

These crops are also well worth growing but require a little more time, protection or space.

◀ Tomatoes
Look for varieties suitable for growing outdoors and grow up against a very sunny wall for best results. They'll need daily watering if in pots.

◀ Cucumbers
Outdoor varieties such as 'Marketmore' are so prolific and tasty. Peel them for best flavour.

◀ Cabbages and kale
These need to be sown in April into the ground or pots, then moved into their final positions in summer, spaced well apart and covered with mesh to protect them from insects. Kale is especially useful as you can harvest it bit by bit through winter.

◀ Parsnips
Can be sown at the same time as carrots, but they can be very slow to germinate and need lots of space.

◀ Peas and mangetout
Can be sown direct where they are to grow or started off in pots. They grow well but are popular with slugs, snails, birds and mice so will need a little protection until they get going, plus plenty of water if it's dry.

◀ Broad beans
Sown in autumn or spring, these need quite a bit of space and you will have to keep an eye out for blackfly in summer.

◀ Leeks
Need to be sown in April into the ground and moved into their final position in July, dropped into little holes so that the stems stay white. They may also need covering to protect from insects.

◀ Squash
Summer squash are very like courgettes. Winter squash are delicious and store well, but need lots of space to grow. One of the tastiest varieties is grey-blue skinned 'Crown Prince'.

Once you've mastered these veg, there are so many more to try including cauliflower, celeriac, bulb fennel, spinach, sweetcorn, pak choi and other oriental leaves, as well as onions, garlic and shallots. For mild areas, you could also experiment with sweet potatoes, tomatillo (*Physalis ixocarpa*) for making into Mexican salsas and cape gooseberries (*Physalis peruviana*) for eating raw or decorating cocktails and puddings.

Edible flowers

Great fun to harvest, and guaranteed to bring smiles from friends and family, edible flowers are easy to grow yet hard to find and expensive to buy in the shops. Many, such as daisies, pinks, violas, lavender and roses can simply be harvested from your borders, but some are annuals that are worth growing in the veg patch. Only pick flowers from plants you have grown yourself, not from plants recently bought which may have pesticide residues. Classic favourites include bright orange nasturtiums and marigolds and bright blue cornflowers and borage.

Greenhouse Growing

Greenhouses are frequently offered for sale second-hand, but you'll usually need to find someone to help you dismantle and rebuild in your garden. The frame will need to stand on fairly solid foundations, such as reclaimed concrete blocks. The whole base does not need to be concrete – in fact, it's far better for growing if you have beds within the greenhouse to plant directly into the soil. To make a solid path along the middle you can simply firm and level the ground and place a few slabs straight on the soil.

As described in Chapter 3 (see page 100), heating a greenhouse is not very sustainable as glass doesn't hold heat well. If you really want heat for propagation, you could run a power supply to your greenhouse and just use it for a heated propagator or bench. This will reduce the length of time seeds take to germinate or cuttings to put down roots. However, even a completely cold greenhouse can be in use all year. Hardy crops like salads can be sown in there from early spring; more tender crops can be grown from mid-spring; heat-loving crops like tomatoes, chillies, peppers, aubergines, cucumbers and melons can fill it during the summer; and then in autumn more hardy crops like spinach, rocket, lettuce, sweet peas and broad beans can be sown for early harvests in spring. It will also provide a little protection for any less hardy ornamental plants you might grow in pots in your garden such as salvias, lemon verbena or *Melianthus major*. These don't mind a bit of cold but need protection from winter wet.

▶ The small greenhouse near the vegetable garden at Bateman's, East Sussex.

Growing tomatoes under glass

Tomatoes in the UK are far more successful if grown in a greenhouse where they will start fruiting earlier, ripen their fruit more quickly and for longer and, crucially, avoid the spores of a fungal disease known as blight, which are carried in damp air outside from summer into autumn. It pays to grow a range of tomatoes – cherries are usually the sweetest and most prolific, but it's nice to have some larger tomatoes for slicing. Look for cordon types (also known as indeterminate), which are trained up against a pole or string, spaced about 50 centimetres apart.

If you have a heated propagator in your greenhouse or a sunny windowsill at home, you can sow your tomato seeds in late February, and then pot up the individual seedlings and keep them somewhere sunny but frost free until it's time to plant them. This can be a little tricky, as an unheated greenhouse may get too cold at times, while most houses are very warm and seedlings may grow a bit leggy reaching for the light. Alternatively buy small plants in early May. Many are available in garden centres, but an even better range is available online or from honesty boxes outside the homes of enthusiastic growers. Look for suppliers who will send them out in plastic-free packaging. If these arrive as small plugs, you can pot them up and grow them on in your greenhouse for a couple of weeks before planting into pots or greenhouse borders in mid-May.

Tomatoes in pots will need very regular watering with liquid feed in it at least once a week; plants in the border will need less water and feed. You'll also need to tie in the main shoot and pinch out sideshoots as they grow – there are useful videos online showing how to do this. They should start fruiting in July and you'll be harvesting non-stop until the end of October.

▲ Goddards, North Yorkshire.

Perennial Veg

If you are very limited for time, growing perennial vegetables that stay in the ground for many years is a good idea as these require minimal feed, water or weeding. There is also the advantage that their cultivation doesn't disturb the soil structure. In permaculture, where the aim is to yield high outputs of food in a sustainable way, perennial crops are highly recommended. Sadly, however, the range is not big.

Be aware that some crops marketed as being perennial, including certain kales, leeks and spinach, may last for a couple of years but are rarely long-lived.

◄ Asparagus
This needs a free-draining soil to do well and will take up quite a bit of space, but once established, each plant will give you several delicious, tender spears each spring. A delicacy which is expensive in the shops.

◄ Yakon
Gaining popularity in the UK, this tuberous plant needs a warm summer and autumn to do well, and protection from winter weather too. Tubers are crunchy and juicy and rarely found in the shops.

◄ Globe artichokes
The part of these huge and beautiful plants which is eaten is the flower buds. They love a sunny, sheltered spot and take up a lot of space, but make a great feature for the corner of a veg garden.

◄ Rhubarb
Usually considered a fruit, rhubarb is a vegetable that grows well in the UK, especially in the colder more northerly parts of the country. It takes a couple of years to establish after planting, but then is usually prolific and can be harvested from spring for many months.

◄ Jerusalem artichokes
Very easy to grow but rather too vigorous and a bit of an acquired taste!

◄ Good King Henry
Not related to spinach but tasting quite like it, this plant can be grown in sun or light shade. Leaves and new shoots are best eaten while young and not too bitter, either raw or cooked.

Herbs

Growing your own herbs is a really rewarding thing to do and something that seriously cuts down food miles, cost and plastic packaging.

Perennial herbs are best planted in a sunny border close to the kitchen. Easy options include bay, rosemary, sage, thyme, lovage, fennel, chives, Welsh onions and oregano. Many people grow these in pots but all will do better if allowed to get their roots down somewhere constantly moist. Lemon verbena is the exception; this is best kept in a pot so it can be moved somewhere dry and sheltered in winter. Ginger and lemongrass can also be grown in pots, but will need a frost-free greenhouse to overwinter, and the energy used for this is unlikely to justify the size of the harvest. Mint is also perennial but is best planted in a shadier spot – keep an eye on it, as once happy it can spread quickly. Many people plant it in a pot sunk into the ground to prevent it spreading.

Many of our best loved culinary herbs are annuals or biennials, which are a bit more complicated as they need to be treated like a vegetable crop. These include:

◀ Basil

Sweet basil, also known as Genovese basil, is the classic large-leafed type, which is perfect for tomato salads, sauces and all Mediterranean recipes. Thai basil with its distinct aniseed flavour is also useful. Sow indoors or in the greenhouse once the nights are warm. Plant out in early summer or plant in a greenhouse border. Basil will grow in pots but only if you water religiously.

◀ Parsley

This germinates best once the soil is warm, but you can pour boiling water on the soil, or compost before sowing. You can also buy a plant from the garden centre or even the supermarket, split up the seedlings and plant them. Parsley will sometimes last through the winter – especially if you cover it with fleece or cloches – but then it will flower in spring and stop producing useful leaves.

◀ Dill

So useful for potato salad, dill needs warmth to germinate, moisture to grow and is very popular with slugs and snails, so is best sown in April once the ground is warm, watered often and kept slug free.

◀ Coriander

This herb from Asia needs warm soil and consistent moisture and is prone to running to seed if it gets hot and dry. Sow in April and again in August (as the days shorten and cool). Pick as soon as it's leafy enough to use.

Storing leafy herbs

Rosemary, bay, thyme and sage will give you a few leaves all year round, but most leafy herbs will be unavailable from autumn until the following summer, so it's a great idea to store them. Most can be chopped and frozen in small, labelled bags. The chopped leaves retain their flavour perfectly for stirring into stews and curries whenever you need them. This technique is especially useful for dill and coriander, which need to be harvested while they are leafy, and not left to go to flower. For basil, you can also blend with oil and salt and freeze in small quantities for adding to many dishes, or making into pesto.

FRUIT

Growing your own fruit is incredibly rewarding and often allows you to have much riper, tastier crops than anything you can buy, without packaging or fear of pesticide residues. Many fruits also store well for use at different times of year, meaning you don't have to rely on unsustainable imports.

Strawberries are one of the most popular fruits, and growing your own means you can try a far wider range of flavoursome varieties than those available in the shops. Strawberries grow well in most UK gardens, especially if the soil has had compost incorporated, and weeds are kept away. The ripe fruits are very popular with birds, mice,

▼ Rather than cultivating fruit you may just decide to allow some blackberries to grow along a wild edge.

slugs and snails, so they may need to be grown in a raised bed and covered with netting for some months of the year. If you don't have the time and space for this, little alpine strawberries are easier and will grow almost anywhere in the garden, even among flower borders.

Raspberries are also really popular and do well in the UK. There are varieties that fruit in summer and others that fruit in autumn. They both need support, but summer canes need to be tied individually to supporting wires whereas autumn varieties such as 'Polka' are by far the easiest, as they just get cut down at the end of winter and new canes can be supported as a whole clump. Loganberries and tayberries are also strong and highly productive plants. They need pruning and training to keep them under control, which simply involves cutting back all the fruited growth when harvesting finishes in late summer, and tying in new growth that will fruit the

following year. The fruits are a bit sour to eat raw but they're useful for puddings and jams. That said, neither are any more useful or delicious than our wild blackberry, so you may prefer to save your energy for blackberry picking in autumn. Raw raspberries, blackberries, tayberries and loganberries freeze really well for use throughout the year. It's so satisfying in winter to be able to blend a handful into a smoothie.

Bush fruits such as gooseberries and currants were once the staple of most allotments, but they're now losing popularity, perhaps because they are less good eaten raw and need a lot of sugar when cooked. To get around this, try blackcurrant varieties such as 'Big Ben', which are sweet and juicy enough to eat raw, and try leaving gooseberries to ripen fully on the bush so they get softer and sweeter. Gooseberries and redcurrants can be trained flat against fences to take up less space; blackcurrants

Orchards

If you are lucky enough to have space for a few fruit trees, orchards can be amazingly sustainable, biodiverse and multi-functioning spaces. Britain used to have many small, traditional orchards, but almost 80 per cent have been lost since 1900. Older orchards with mature trees containing dead wood are especially valuable as wildlife habitat. Such trees still fruit prolifically but apples are often small and out of reach; if you are lucky enough to have one, consider making juice or cider rather than trying to wrestle it back to size. The National Trust looks after many different types of orchard, including some containing historic varieties – as at Cotehele (pictured) in Cornwall – and is helping to plant many more in rural and urban sites.

can't. Jostaberries, which are a hybrid between gooseberries and blackcurrants, take up a lot of space but are attractive and have multi-purpose fruit. Blueberries are far trickier, needing an acid soil and plenty of water. Unless your soil has a naturally low pH (see page 70), these are best grown in pots of loam-based ericaceous compost, and given daily watering in summer, with netting to keep the birds away from ripening fruit.

Tree fruit such as apples, pears and plums take up more space, but they are very attractive garden trees that provide nectar and pollen for insects, and sometimes welcome shade for us. It is also possible to keep apple and pear trees quite small by buying them on dwarfing rootstocks and even training them flat against walls and fences. Cherries are very tempting, but rarely worth the hassle as birds tend to find the fruit long before they have ripened, and netting a tree can be awkward.

◀ Raspberries, like these ones ripening at Ickworth in Suffolk, are a popular fruit and do well in the UK.

EATING YOUR OWN PRODUCE ALL YEAR ROUND

If you have already grown vegetables for a few seasons, you'll know all about summer and autumn gluts, and then the hungry gap when winter veg run out and very little else is ready until May or June. This is hard to avoid due to our temperate climate when winter light levels and temperatures are just not conducive to growth. The art of handling this involves sowing in small batches, as late and as early as you dare, getting the hang of storing surplus and embracing seasonal eating.

Successional Sowing

For crops such as lettuce, spinach and salad rocket, which you want throughout the year but which are prone to bolting, sow little and often. With lettuce especially, you really only need a pinch of seed every three weeks from April to August.

If you have a greenhouse or cold frame you can do your last sowings of these salads as late as September, either direct into the soil or in large pots, for small harvests during autumn. Some seedlings may even limp through the winter and get going again in early spring for useful harvests then. Oriental leaves, rocket and baby leaf kale are especially good at overwintering. After the worst of winter, a greenhouse is also very useful for early sowings of these same hardy crops, along with others like peas and spring onions, so they are ready to plant outside once the ground has warmed up a bit. Sowing in lengths of gutter can mean you have whole rows of seedlings ready to go out with minimal disturbance to their roots.

◄ Colourful chard and pumpkins growing in the kitchen garden at Beningbrough, Yorkshire, in autumn.

Expert gardeners sometimes make two sowings of cucumbers and courgettes, so that in July when their spring-sown plants are past their best, they can rip them out and replant with ones sown in early summer. Dwarf French beans may also benefit from being sown in two batches, a month apart, to have beans for as long as possible. Carrots sown all at the same time can simply be harvested at different sizes, but you'll get great results from sowing different types for early and later cropping.

Crops for the hungry gap

If you are determined to have some fresh produce in the garden every month, there are key crops which will serve you well in the tricky period of February, March and April. Parsnips, leeks and kale sown in spring can be left in the ground right through winter for harvesting into the start of the following year, but keep an eye on them, as left too long they will begin to produce flowers and become less palatable. Purple sprouting broccoli (shown above) is grown specifically for its flowering shoots, which will develop as soon as the days begin to lengthen in late winter. If you have space for perennials like rhubarb and asparagus, these can be harvested from March for a few months.

▶ Many crops can be preserved for use in the future and it's lovely to have a store cupboard full of these.

Storing Produce

Storing produce will allow you to make use of gluts and have something home-grown in all your meals, meaning you're cutting down on imports and trips to the shops.

Some produce such as squash, onions, garlic, apples and maincrop potatoes can be stored fresh for months if simply kept in a cool, dry place. The key is to ensure they are fully dry before you store them and to check stores every now and again to throw out anything showing signs

of mould. Different apple varieties store better than others, with some needing to be eaten soon after harvest, others lasting through to Christmas and a few staying firm even longer in the right conditions.

Freezing is a good option for many other crops, preserving lots of their nutrients. If you have a half-empty freezer, it'll use very little extra energy to fill it up with produce that saves you shopping. Most soft fruit freezes well raw, while apples, pears, plums and rhubarb are better stewed first. Beans are best blanched in hot water before freezing; tomatoes made into sauce. All these things are so useful to have at home for making a last-minute pudding or pasta.

Pickling and preserving is an art that many keen veg growers choose to master. Beetroot slices, mini-cucumbers, radishes, chunks of

on how easily they set and whether you need to add a source of pectin to help. Jam uses a huge amount of sugar so you might not eat a lot of it, but having some jars spare is lovely for giving away to friends. If you don't pick enough fruit in one go to make jam, you can freeze each day's harvest for a week or so until you have enough and then make it on a rainy day.

Seasonal Eating

Even if you remember to sow little and often, you are still likely to have periods where a certain crop is really prolific and needs to be eaten regularly for a few weeks, or given away to friends, neighbours or community food projects. The idea of eating the same vegetable almost every day is unthinkable to many people today as they have got used to year-round access to a wide variety of vegetables from all over the world. However, with a bit of imaginative cooking, it's easy to avoid it becoming boring. There's also something special about really relishing a crop while it's in its prime, knowing that once it is finished, it won't be available again for several months.

Even if you only grow a few herbs or a little veg, or don't have space or time to grow at all, you can try to eat seasonally and celebrate what's in season. Seasonal British crops will have been transported far shorter distances and are more likely to have been grown to the standards we expect in terms of pesticide residues, water consumption, land use and conditions for workers. It's also really fun to visit farm shops and buy strawberries, asparagus, new potatoes, pumpkins or whatever delicacy is having its peak at that moment.

Learning the art of putting vegetables at the centre of a meal is also great, whether you have a plant-based diet or simply wish to eat healthily. There is widespread agreement that eating meat with every meal is not good for us or the planet.

parsnip and cauliflower florets are all delicious pickled so that they last for many months. Courgettes, beetroots, green tomatoes, green beans, plums and apples also make great chutney. All fruits can be made into jam, they'll just vary

▲ Harvesting is one of the greatest pleasures of vegetable growing.

▼▼ Season of mists and mellow fruitfulness – and for veg gardeners, perhaps the autumn glut.

LOOKING AFTER THE SOIL IN A VEG PLOT

Soil health underpins success in the vegetable garden where crops need to develop good root systems in order to grow the lush leaves, tender stems, fleshy tubers or plump fruit we want to eat. Strong root systems and associated soil biology are also key to a plant's ability to withstand attack from pests and diseases. However, growing and harvesting annual crops on the same patch of land means nutrients are constantly being taken from the soil to feed us and need to be replenished. Uprooting plants, digging over a bed and leaving it bare between crops also affects soil structure and biology.

No Dig Gardening

One approach to soil health, which is now firmly established and used by many National Trust gardeners, is 'no dig' or, at least, minimal dig. This is a move away from the once-traditional approach to managing a veg plot, which saw gardeners routinely dig over empty beds in autumn or winter and leave them bare so that any insect pests in the soil were exposed to birds, and winter frosts would help break up heavy soils to make them more friable. These days it is considered preferable in most cases to leave the soil as undisturbed as possible, protecting the natural structure and allowing soil micro-organisms to build healthy communities. In no dig gardening, when crops are harvested, the bare soil is covered with a layer of well-rotted compost and the next crops are sown or planted straight into it. The mulch protects the soil surface, buries weed seeds, feeds soil micro-organisms, increases fertility and improves its

▶ Some digging and careful site preparation is often needed to get a veg plot set up but after that it's best to avoid disturbing the soil structure.

No dig gardening at Clumber

The team at Clumber Park have been practising no dig since 2016 when they first experimented with the technique. This approach has helped improve the fertility and moisture retention on their sandy soil, meaning they never use fertiliser, and rarely have to water to produce great quality crops. They make their own compost for mulching the beds each year. It's heavy work for the team putting it onto the beds each year but they save a lot of time by not having to weed or water as much in spring and summer.

▼ Kitchen Garden, Clumber Park, Nottinghamshire.

moisture-holding capacity. It also saves a lot of backbreaking work for us gardeners. By not disturbing soil, less carbon is released into the atmosphere. In no dig gardening, defined beds with paths between them are used to ensure soil is not walked on, further helping its structure.

Key to success with this approach is having a really good composting system set up so that you are producing all the compost required for mulching. Buying in compost or manure for vegetable gardens is far less sustainable and may mean you accidentally introduce unwanted chemicals or microplastics.

Winter Cover

While keeping soil covered with mulches is far preferable to leaving it bare, having living plants growing in the soil at all times is now understood to be the best way to keep soil biology healthy and prevent leaching of nutrients. Ways to keep roots in the ground as much as possible in vegetable gardens include using green manures and growing winter hardy crops. Even just leaving weeds that have germinated in autumn in bare patches until spring when you need the ground again, may have some benefits.

Green manures are crops such as *Phacelia tanacetifolia*, winter field beans (*Vicia faba*), common vetch (*Vicia sativa*) and crimson clover, which you can sow in late summer or early autumn, leave over the winter and then dig in the following spring before planting your vegetables. Plants in the pea and bean family (such as beans and clover) are especially good as they fix nitrogen from the air and store it in little nodules in their roots, which are then dug into the soil, fertilising it. The only challenges of green manures are that crops which are tough enough to get through the winter can be quite hard work to dig in, unless you have machinery,

and obviously digging is now thought to be very disruptive to soil structure and biology.

Crops that you can leave in the ground through winter include kale, purple sprouting broccoli, leeks, winter cabbages, parsnips, over-wintering broad beans, plus chard and parsley. The latter two do best in cold areas if you cover them with fleece or cloches.

▲ Don't be in a hurry to tidy up in winter, leaving your soil exposed to the weather.

MAINTAINING HEALTHY CROPS

As described in Chapter 4 (see page 137), there is a welcome change happening in horticulture as we realise that labelling the creatures that share our gardens as 'pests', and trying to eliminate them, is not sustainable. Increasingly, we want our gardens to be safe havens for wildlife, and are willing to tolerate the odd maggot in a homegrown plum or hole in a potato. However,

there is no denying the frustration of coming out into the vegetable garden after a damp night to discover an entire row of newly planted lettuces demolished by slugs and snails, or finding pigeons have ripped your kale to shreds in one sitting. At times, defending against these things and recovering from attacks can be very stressful, which is not good for our relationship with the natural world or our well-being.

Many advocates of nature-friendly gardening claim that with the right mindset and beneficial creatures in your garden, everything can be done in perfect harmony with nature. While this may be possible in an ornamental garden, it is quite a challenge in the veg patch. Today's crops are not wild plants with natural resistance; they are the result of centuries of breeding to make them sweet, juicy and tender – characteristics which mean they are highly attractive to other species and sometimes more vulnerable to disease. Man has also been growing the same few crops around the world in large quantities for a long time, creating an imbalance whereby insects or diseases which are adapted to them are widespread.

Fortunately, there is much that can be achieved by good gardening practices. Strong plants hardened off before planting out will withstand attack far better than soft, sappy ones straight from the garden centre or greenhouse. Seeds and plants planted into moist, fertile soil will put down roots quicker and build greater resilience to drought, insect attack or disease. Tidiness is probably more important in the vegetable garden than elsewhere in a nature-friendly garden. While habitat for attracting pollinators and other beneficial insects is welcome nearby, it is unwise to allow for places in the vegetable garden where slugs and snails can hide during the day and easily access your beds at night.

◄ Most vegetable growers experience different crop successes and failures each year but usually have plenty to harvest in summer and autumn.

Knowledge is Power

When you do spot a problem, try to research
what it is. Use a trusted pest and disease
identification guide or website such as the Royal
Horticultural Society's. Sometimes you may be
able to tolerate an aphid infestation and still get
a crop, or cut off the worst affected leaves and
increase watering to slow the spread of powdery
mildew. Understanding the life cycle of the
pathogens your crops are prone to can help you
time your sowing in future years. Flea beetles
on rocket are rarely a problem with the cool,
moist conditions of spring and autumn, but are
terrible in mid-summer; blackfly on broad beans
is far less of a problem in plants that were sown
in autumn and are already forming pods when
the blackfly appears in May. Carrots sown after
mid-May and harvested before the end of August
can avoid attack from the carrot root fly; early
potatoes harvested before mid-July should escape
potato blight. Sometimes you may even have to
break the cycle by not growing a particular crop
for a few years.

Covering crops after you sow or plant them
is often the best bet. Cabbages, cauliflowers,
broccoli and kale are all popular with large and
small white butterflies, whitefly and pigeons,
while ripening strawberries are beloved by slugs
and snails, birds and small mammals, especially
squirrels. Netting carrots can stop carrot root fly
and netting leeks may stop leek moth and allium
leaf miner. The fine netting which is best for
keeping out many of these predators is expensive
and plastic-based so it's a good idea to ensure
the supports you hang it over allow for it to be
put up and taken down year after year without
making holes in it.

▶ A good example of the use of fine protective
netting in the garden of Wimpole Hall in
Cambridgeshire; carefully supported like this,
it can be redeployed season after season.

Companion Planting

Companion planting involves deliberately planting one species close to another to provide benefits, such as luring an insect pest away, or preventing it finding a crop you want to protect. Many companion plants have attractive flowers, making veg plots look really pretty so it is a popular and frequently adopted approach, even if its benefits are not always fully proven.

Commonly tried companion planting includes growing highly scented plants like marigolds and herbs near cabbages to prevent insects such as large white and small white butterflies and flea beetles from locating the crops to lay their eggs. Interspersing rows of carrots with rows of onions, garlic, shallots or spring onion may also help disguise their smell so that carrot root fly never finds them. Planting French marigolds (*Tagetes* spp.) in your greenhouse may help deter whitefly from the tomatoes. Planting nasturtiums near cabbage or kale may encourage cabbage white butterflies to bypass your crops and lay their eggs on them instead. Planting almost any flowers among beans may lure in female hoverflies to feed and they might then lay their eggs among the aphids on the beans so the resulting larvae can eat the aphids.

In reality, all gardens are made up of a mix of plants, so some beneficial relationships are usually going on without careful planning. Almost any flowers in borders near your veg plot will be providing for creatures that may go on to have a positive impact on your crops.

Attracting beneficial creatures

Although a perfect equilibrium between pests and their predators may be too much to expect in a vegetable garden, attracting beneficial creatures into your garden by providing suitable habitat will definitely make some difference. Frogs, toads, newts and some birds do eat slugs and snails. Ladybird larvae (pictured) are voracious consumers of aphids, as are blue tits. Earwigs eat aphids and many other pests on fruit trees, more than they eat fruit. As outlined in Chapter 2 (page 64), gardeners also rely on insects to pollinate some crops, including courgettes, cucumbers, squash, fruit trees and currants.

◀ Marigolds mixed with cabbages – a demonstration of tried and tested 'companion planting' in the kitchen garden at Avebury Manor in Wiltshire.

CONCLUSION: FEELING GOOD IN YOUR GARDEN

Those of us who garden regularly do so because of the benefits it provides. It gets us out in the fresh air, builds muscles, improves dexterity and burns calories; it gives us something to concentrate on, nurture and feel proud of. Being outside in nature is thought to combat feelings of loneliness and depression, while chatting about plants with friends and neighbours, taking on an allotment or getting involved in a community garden are great ways to build friendships. Research also suggests that gardening is good for our health because it releases hormones, which can improve brain function, and exposes us to bacteria in the soil that can support our gut biome and boost our mood.

Some of these incredible benefits can be undone if gardening ever feels like a battle with nature, or a waste of time or money. So it makes sense to stop striving for impossible levels of order, resist impulse buys and choose plants and materials carefully. Gardening with wildlife in mind helps us to take a more mindful approach. Instead of rushing to complete tasks, it encourages us to stop and look at what's there. Watching the creatures that share our gardens is so good for the soul, helping us to slow down, be gentle and appreciate the beauty and intricacy all around. Taking action to encourage new creatures into the garden and seeing it work is awe-inspiring, showing us nature can thrive if given the chance. We gardeners have the power to make a big difference to the lives of individual creatures and, collectively, to whole species.

If you have the space to grow your own food, or be part of a community project, that can also be really empowering. Eating what you grow can save you money, be great for your health and teach you about what's in season. Added to this, when friends come for a meal or you take a cake into work, nothing makes for a better talking point than being able to say you grew some of the ingredients yourself!

Our ability to garden is part of our success as a species, but so too is our ability to adapt to changing circumstances. Let's not allow tradition or convenience stop us from learning how to garden in a way that is good for us and for our environment. Our gardens are the one small piece of the planet that we have the power to protect. It's time to stop admiring them for how manicured they look and start to welcome a little wildness close to our homes.

▶ Don't forget to stop and sit and admire your garden and its wildlife once in a while.

CREDITS

Recommended reading: *The Garden Jungle: or Gardening to Save the Planet* by Dave Goulson (Jonathan Cape, 2019); *Wildlife of a Garden: A Thirty-year Study* by Jennifer Owen (Royal Horticultural Society, 2010).

ACKNOWLEDGEMENTS

This book would not have been possible without input from many of the brilliant gardeners, ecologists and champions of sustainability in the National Trust. Particular thanks go to Caroline Gettinby, Alison Pringle and Felicity Roos.

Thanks also to Andrew Salisbury and others at the RHS for their excellent research and to Kevin Peberdy, Sally Mackenzie and others connected to wetland conservation for the inspiration they provide.

Thanks to Clare Savage, Charlotte Mozley and Jenny Bevan for proof-reading. Credit, above all, must go to Rich Hearn, my partner and an incredible ornithologist who inspired me to write this book and passed away before it was finished.

◀ Burnet moth on *Allium sphaerocephalon*.